Lucill T.
March 8, 2015
Calgary

PROCLUS
On Providence

PROCLUS
On Providence

Translated by
Carlos Steel

Cornell University Press

Ithaca, New York

© 2007 by Carlos Steel

All rights reserved. Except for brief
quotations in a review, this book, or parts
thereof, must not be reproduced in any form
without permission in writing from the publisher.
For information address Cornell University Press,
Sage House, 512 East State Street, Ithaca, New York 14850.

First published 2007 by Cornell University Press.

ISBN 978-0-8014-4533-0

Acknowledgments

The present translations have been made possible by generous and imaginative funding from the following sources: the National Endowment for the Humanities, Division of Research Programs, an independent federal agency of the USA; the Leverhulme Trust; the British Academy; the Jowett Copyright Trustees; the Royal Society (UK); Centro Internazionale A. Beltrame di Storia dello Spazio e del Tempo (Padua); Mario Mignucci; Liverpool University; the Leventis Foundation; the Arts and Humanities Research Council; Gresham College; the Esmée Fairbairn Charitable Trust; the Henry Brown Trust; Mr and Mrs N. Egon; the Netherlands Organisation for Scientific Research (NWO/GW); Dr Victoria Solomonides, the Cultural Attaché of the Greek Embassy in London. The editor wishes to thank John Sellars for preparing the volume for press, and Deborah Blake at Duckworth, who has been the publisher responsible for every volume since the first.

Printed and bound in Great Britain

Librarians: Library of Congress Cataloging-in-
Publication Data are available.

Contents

Conventions	vi
Preface	vii
Introduction	1
Translation	39
Notes	73
Philological Appendix	93
Bibliography	111
Index of Passages	117
Index of Names	119
Index of Subjects	121

Conventions

[…] Square brackets enclose words or phrases that have been added to the translation or the lemmata for purposes of clarity.

<…> Angle brackets enclose conjectures relating to the Greek text, i.e. additions to the transmitted text deriving from parallel sources and editorial conjecture, and transposition of words or phrases. Accompanying notes provide further details.

(…) Round brackets, besides being used for ordinary parentheses, contain transliterated Greek words.

Preface

Queris autem milesies dicta (1,10)

Proclus' reply to Theodore offers one of the most remarkable discussions on fate, providence, and free choice in Late Antiquity. It continues a long debate that had started with the first polemics of the Platonists against the Stoic doctrine of determinism. How can there be room for free choice and moral responsibility in a world governed by an unalterable fate? Notwithstanding its great interest, Proclus' reply to Theodore has not received the attention from scholars it deserves, probably because its text is not very accessible to the modern reader. It has survived together with the two other *opuscula* in a medieval Latin translation and, in large extracts, in a Byzantine compilation. For a general presentation of the *opuscula*, their complex text tradition, and the principles of translation, the reader is referred to the introduction of *On the Existence of Evils*, which I published with Jan Opsomer in this same series in 2003.

As Plato says in the *Laws* (IV 709B-C), three factors play a role in the accomplishment of a human work. God governs all human affairs directing them to the good, next come fortune and right moment (*kairos*). As a third factor after these two comes the skill of the agent. Let me therefore first thank Richard Sorabji as the providential cause of this enterprise for accepting this second Proclus volume in the framework of the Ancient Commentators on Aristotle. I include in my thanks the project's editorial assistant, John Sellars. Secondly, I have to praise the 'good fortune' that I could prepare this translation in the De Wulf-Mansion Centre in Leuven, which not only offers wonderful research facilities, but is above all a dynamic community of scholars in ancient and medieval thought: I thank my colleagues Gerd Van Riel, Russell Friedman, and my younger collaborators Leen Van Campe, Pieter d'Hoine and Christoph Helmig. I have to thank in particular John Dudley, who spent hours in the library meticulously correcting an intermediate draft of my translation. He allowed me to avoid many errors and greatly improved the style of the translation. When I had finished a first draft of my translation, I met Benedikt Strobel at a Proclus conference in Jena, who provided me with a Greek retroversion of the Latin translation of Proclus' treatise. Since then we have had an intensive correspondence leading to ever further corrections. The quality of this final version would not have been possible without the help of this retroversion. A version of the translation was used at a colloquium organized by the Academia Platonica at the University of Leiden in autumn 2005. It was a great privilege to discuss Proclus' treatise with this group of Platonic scholars. I thank Frans De Haas, John Dillon, Luc Brisson, Jens Halfwassen and all the other participants.

In a letter to Erasmus (1525) Floriano Montini asks his learned friend if he could provide him with a copy of Proclus' work *De fato*. 'The text which I found at Rome was full of errors. As his essay shows, Proclus was a man of wide learning with a deep interest in religion. In the essay which he wrote for Theodorus on the working of providence, which contains a discussion of the problem of free will and destiny, he put forward many subtle arguments and clarified many points, though the subject is generally perplexing and difficult. So I would appreciate it greatly if you would help me to read these essays in a more accurate text' (Letter 1552, *Collected Works of Erasmus*, vol. 11, pp. 47-8, trans. A. Dalzell). Erasmus did not reply. He had no copy, and even if he had had one, it is not sure that Montini would have been much helped by it. His problem in understanding was not due to the bad copy, but to the problems with the Latin of Moerbeke. We hope that this first English translation of Proclus' treatise may help us to read Proclus' arguments – almost lost in the precarious transmission of the text – 'in a more accurate text'. They deserve it, for 'they are about problems that have been discussed a thousand times and will never cease to challenge us to investigate them' (1,10-11).

Carlos Steel

Introduction

I. Proclus' reply to Theodore the engineer

1. The treatise in the work of Proclus

Among the works of Proclus (412-85) three treatises are devoted to problems of providence, fate, free choice, and evil. The first treatise examines ten different problems that were commonly discussed in the Platonic school. The third is the celebrated treatise on the existence of evil, which, through the adaptation of Dionysius the Areopagite, had a great fortune in the medieval tradition, both at Byzantium and in the Latin West. The second is of a particular literary genre. It is a reply to a letter that a certain Theodore, an engineer, had written to Proclus. In this letter Theodore had put forward a number of arguments in favour of determinism. Although Theodore could discuss all these matters with friends at home, he seeks advice from Proclus, the leading philosophical authority of his time, and besides 'an old friend' who could not refuse to answer. Proclus does not have much sympathy for the views defended by Theodore and considers most of his arguments simplistic. Nevertheless, the questions Theodore raises on fate and self-determination are so important that they deserve a long discussion. Proclus' reply, though addressed to Theodore, is intended to be read by a wider philosophical audience. In it, Proclus develops in a clear, accessible style his views on fate and providence, on the soul, on the levels of knowledge, and above all on the possibility and limits of human freedom. As we shall see, the treatise continues the long debate that had started with the first polemics of the Academy against the Stoic deterministic worldview.

Proclus composed the treatise in his later career, as can be inferred from some indications in the text. Theodore introduces himself as an 'old friend' who seeks contact after many years. Proclus himself gives the impression of being already an older man. For when discussing Theodore's hedonistic views, he declares that such a view is unworthy of his old age (45,4). In chapter 22, Proclus seems to refer to a dramatic event in his life that was also known to Theodore, since he mentioned it in his letter: 'for also the accidents that, as you mentioned, recently came over us from outside, have deprived us of walls and stones, my friend, and have reduced wooden beams to ashes, all of which are mortal and inflammable things, and have ruined our wealth'. According to Westerink, Proclus may be alluding here to some persecution he suffered. The destruction by Christians of the temple of Asclepius, which was adjacent to the school, may have caused serious damage to the school.[1] It may have been this religious persecution that drove Proclus into exile in Lydia. As we know from Marinus, Proclus spent a year in Lydia before it was safe to return to Athens.[2] We do not know when this exile happened, but it must have been when Proclus was already an established scholar. All these indications point to a composition of the treatise later in his life. On the other hand, there are many parallels between this treatise and the discussion of determinism and free choice in the commentary on the *Republic*, in particular in the sixteenth essay, which is devoted to the interpretation of the myth of Er. Of particular interest is the concluding section of this essay (*in Remp.* II 355,8-359,8). After having explained all details of the myth Proclus adds, as a conclusion, the basic elements of the Platonic doctrine on what depends on us, fate and providence: 'Let this be the end of our explanation of the myth! I too shall conclude my essay, but only after adding to the preceding some seminal ideas that may elucidate the doctrine of Plato on what depends on us, on fate and providence' (*in Remp.* II 355,8-11). What follows could be taken as an outline of the views Proclus develops in his reply to Theodore. Even the description of the subject corresponds exactly to the title of the treatise, except, of course, the dedication to Theodore: *peri tou eph' hêmin kai heimarmenês kai pronoias*. It seems that Proclus took the letter of Theodore as an opportunity to compose the treatise 'On what depends on us, on fate and providence' that he had intended to write when working on the *Republic*. Unfortunately, we do not know when the commentary of the *Republic* was composed. In fact, it is not really a commentary, but a collection of seventeen essays on diverse issues related to the *Republic*, which may have been written at different moments. The final composition, however, was written after the 'publication' of the commentary on the *Timaeus*.[3] It seems thus reasonable to place the composition of the *Tria opuscula* some years after Proclus had finished the redaction of the commentary on the *Republic*.[4]

Notwithstanding its great philosophical interest, Proclus' reply to Theodore has not received the attention from scholars it deserves, probably because its text is not very accessible to the modern reader. It has survived in a Latin medieval translation and, in large extracts, in a Greek compilation by a Byzantine prince philosopher from the early twelfth century, Isaac Sebastokrator.[5] In 1960, Helmut Boese published the Latin text of the three treatises together with a partial reconstruction of the lost Greek, based mainly on the extracts preserved by Isaac Sebastokrator. In 1979, Daniel Isaac provided a new edition of the Latin text with a French annotated translation and an edition of the corresponding Greek treatise of Sebastokrator.[6] Also in 1979, Michael Erler published the treatise of Sebastokrator and, in 1980, a German translation of Proclus' treatise.[7] The modern translations are helpful, but suffer from an insufficient knowledge of the manner in which Moerbeke translated Proclus' Greek text.[8] My translation aims at rendering the original Greek text of Proclus as we can reconstruct it from Moerbeke's translation and from Sebastokrator's paraphrase. I have profited greatly from a reconstruction of the lost Greek text prepared by Benedikt Strobel. Whenever in the translation I depart from the Latin text, as published by Boese, I offer a justification in the Philological Appendix at the end of this volume.

2. Theodore the engineer

We have no other information on this Theodore than what we can infer from Proclus' reply. Theodore is not a philosopher by profession, but an engineer (*mêkhanikos*). Throughout the treatise Proclus refers, often ironically and in an *ad hominem* argument, to the scientific expertise of Theodore who is 'well trained in the mathematical and geometrical sciences' (41,3-5). He calls arithmetic and geometry 'the mother of his discipline' (18,10). After having explained how Theodore understands the universe as a mechanical clock, Proclus notices ironically: 'Perhaps you have entertained such views to honour your own discipline, considering the maker of the universe to be some kind of engineer and yourself as the imitator of the best of all causes' (2,19-21). Theodore the engineer as the imitator of the great demiurge of the world! And, at the end, in chapter 65, Proclus refers to Theodore's construction of an astronomical calendar (*parapêgma*), which makes uses of wheels and pins. Even a famous saying of Archimedes is used as an argument against the engineer: 'For you should not think that the often quoted words "to move with a given force a given weight" applies only to you [engineers]: it applies even more to those who live according to virtue to adorn the power given from the universe with another power that is truly a power' (25,18-22).

Theodore introduces himself as an old acquaintance of Proclus. He is probably not a close friend, and it seems that both men have not seen each other in many years. Theodore is acquainted with the Athenian Neoplatonic School, since Proclus assumes that the names of Plotinus and Iamblichus sound familiar to him. And even Theodore of Asine is not a stranger to him. Otherwise he would not have understood the indirect reference Proclus makes to Theodore in 53,13 calling him 'your namesake'. In his conclusion, Proclus refers to his beloved master Syrianus without naming him (66,6), which again suggests that Theodore must have known that Syrianus was Proclus' teacher and must have remembered what he 'used to say'. Moreover, Theodore knows the basic tenets of the Platonic doctrine. From all this evidence one may conclude that Theodore spent some time in the school of Athens together with Proclus, maybe as a disciple of Syrianus, around 435, two years before the death of the latter in 437.[9]

Although it is evident that Theodore had his education in a Platonic school, he is certainly not a Platonist as regards his own philosophy. This engineer, an educated lay philosopher as it were, seems to have professed a remarkably idiosyncratic philosophy, a mixture of views one may sometimes find in a department of engineering among scientists with some philosophical interest. As we shall see, Theodore defends a radical determinism that leaves no place for free choice. At first sight, his views on fate and providence seem to have been inspired by the Stoic doctrine. He understands the world as a fully deterministic system and identifies the inescapable necessity, which governs all events, with providence. On one essential point, however, he differs from Stoicism. Notwithstanding their deterministic worldview, the Stoics always defended the possibility of free choice. Their philosophical opponents all argued that this position was self-contradictory. If all events are necessarily connected and the soul is itself a physical entity, it seems to follow that the celebrated power 'that depends on us' is only an empty word, but nothing in reality. Theodore, however, fully accepts this consequence, against which the Stoics protested. Everything in this world is necessitated, and it is an illusion to believe that we have free choice. As we shall see, many of Theodore's arguments for determinism come from Stoic sources, but they have been radicalised. Other arguments come from the sceptical tradition of the Academy, some even have a hedonistic flavour. This mixture would rather characterise an amateur eclectic philosopher.[10]

The name of Theodore reminds us of the famous Theodore, the geometer, who is introduced by Plato in the *Theaetetus*. Could it be that the Theodore of Proclus is just a fictional character making it possible to write a defence of free choice against a deterministic view represented by an 'engineer'? There are, however, many details in the texts that indicate that we are dealing with a real person with particular views. Proclus attacks Theodore *ad hominem*, he quotes literally from his letter, he follows the series of problems raised by Theodore, although he does not understand why they come in that particular order. There are the references to Theodore ('your namesake'!) and to Syrianus, who indicate that Theodore stayed some time in the school in Athens. Finally Theodore uses a rather idiosyncratic mixture of philosophical arguments (a mechanical determinism expressed in Stoic phrases, with a flavour of hedonism and scepticism). This is characteristic of an individual thinker, who is not a professional philosopher, but puts together his own worldview. For all those reasons we have to admit that Theodore is a real historical character, a pagan intellectual as Proclus himself, but defending views deviating from the then dominant Neoplatonism.

II. The debate on providence, fate and free choice in the imperial period

1. Proclus' sources

The questions Theodore raises about fate and providence are not new. As Proclus says, they have been discussed 'a thousand times', and they will come back again and again, since they will never find a fully satisfactory answer and continue to challenge the soul to investigate them:

> They have indeed already been examined by many: they have been discussed by the famous Plotinus and Iamblichus, and before them in the writings of the divine Plato, as also, if I may express my opinion, before Plato in the revelations made by theologians who proclaimed 'with a delirious mouth' what Plato has established by more sober demonstrations. And what need is there to bring forward Plato and the experts in divine matters? The gods themselves, who know their own affairs clearly and also which and what kind of things they produced after themselves, have openly expressed their views, and not in riddles, as do the theologians.[11]

Proclus here clearly indicates the authorities he intends to follow on providence and fate. (1) His main philosophical authority is Plato, as read and interpreted in the Neoplatonic tradition, in particular by Plotinus, Porphyry and Iamblichus. (2) Proclus also acknowledges the authority of the theologians. Orpheus and Homer do not use 'sober demonstrations' as philosophers do, but speak 'in riddles' and deliver their mythical stories 'with a delirious mouth'. (3) Finally, there is the authority of the gods themselves, who have revealed their views on fate in oracles, in particular in the *Chaldean Oracles*.

The central questions of Proclus' treatise, the relation of fate to providence and the possibility of free choice, had indeed 'been discussed a thousand times', as Proclus admits. They had become dominant themes in the philosophical schools of Late Antiquity, in particular in the polemics against the Stoic view.

2. Stoicism

As is well known, the Stoics understood the physical world as a fully deterministic system wherein all events are governed by fate, which, in their view, is identical with providence.[12] On the other hand, they made the possibility of free choice a central thesis of their ethical doctrine. As Epictetus said, the distinction between what depends on us (*eph' hêmin*) and what does not is the beginning of moral life. What depends on us, is not our body, its health or beauty, nor our richness or poverty, nor our political career, nor our reputation. Only the way we react in our attitudes, our beliefs, our assent, our appraisal, our likes or dislikes, our preference or aversion fully depend on us. However, if the soul is itself of a corporeal nature and so are all its activities and the dispositions it acquires, how could it ever have a capacity of self-determination? How is it possible to maintain human responsibility in a fully deterministic explanation of the universe?

Following Sharples I use here the term 'responsibility' to express the meaning of the complicated Greek phrase *to eph' hêmin*, avoiding thus the term 'free will'. As Sharples rightly observes, the debate in the Hellenistic and post-Hellenistic schools is 'conducted in terms of responsibility rather than of freedom or free will'. 'Freedom is indeed a favourite term of the Stoics, but it is used rather to express the freedom of the wise man whose desires are such that they cannot be hindered by outside interference. Responsibility for actions, however, is something shared by all men, not just by the wise'.[13] The adverbial expression *eph' hêmin* was already used in this sense by Aristotle, though it became popular through Stoicism. In fact, the Stoics insisted as much as their opponents that human agents are responsible for the moral quality of their actions and deserve correspondingly blame or praise. They developed various arguments to show that moral responsibility was not incompatible with physical determinism, introducing distinctions between primarily and auxiliary causes and arguing that our actions make a difference in a causal sequence of events.[14] None of those arguments could, however, convince their opponents; on the contrary, they only fuelled the debate.

The discussion continued in the schools of the imperial period. Now, however, no longer the Stoics, but their opponents, Platonists and Aristotelians, came to dominate the philosophical scene.[15]

3. Middle Platonism

In his *Handbook of Platonism*, Alcinous devotes chapter 26 to an explanation of Plato's doctrine on fate. His starting point is the celebrated myth of Er, which concludes Plato's *Republic*.[16] Er tells how the human souls have to make a choice of life before they are incarnated in bodies. This choice is their own inalienable responsibility. They should not complain later and accuse fate and the gods if they see what events of life follow once they made a wrong choice. In Alcinous' interpretation Plato does not understand fate as an absolute determinism, but as a conditional necessity. The initial choice is not itself determined by fate, but sets the condition for fate. Once taken this decision, the consequences follow inevitably. Therefore Plato insists that 'the responsibility belongs to the one who chooses' (*Resp.* 617E). This doctrine of conditional fate is also found in other authors drawing on middle-Platonic material (such as pseudo-Plutarch, *On Fate*,

Nemesius and Calcidius). Proclus adopted this doctrine in his own explanation of the myth of Er.[17]

In the Stoic view 'providence' must be identified with 'fate'. Both terms have a different meaning: *heimarmenê* indicates the inevitable sequence of events in the chain of causes, *pronoia* indicates that the physical order is the expression of a divine Reason. In reality, however, the providential order is nothing but the necessity of the chain of causes and events. In opposition to this view, the middle-Platonists clearly distinguished fate from providence and subordinated the former to the latter. As Nemesius formulates it: 'all that happens in accordance with fate happens also in accordance with providence, but not all that is in accordance with providence is also in accordance with fate'.[18] Or as Calcidius says: 'fatum ex providentia est nec tamen ex fato providentia'.[19] All later Platonists adopted this view. As we shall see, Proclus makes this distinction one of the three preliminaries of the discussion on providence and fate.

4. Alexander of Aphrodisias

Aristotelian philosophers also entered the debate with Stoic determinism. The most important representative of the Aristotelian tradition is Alexander of Aphrodisias, who composed his treatise *On Fate* around 200.[20] In the first part of this treatise he exposes his own theory of fate, starting from the Aristotelian analysis of causality. Fate is identified with nature. In the Aristotelian understanding of nature, events are never fully determined: they happen in most of the cases, leaving open contingency. In the second part of the treatise, Alexander launches a long polemic against the arguments of the determinists, showing that their doctrine leads to absurd consequences and refuting their arguments in defence of their position. Alexander nowhere in his treatise explicitly identifies his opponents as Stoics. But, as Sharples observes, there can be no doubt that he mainly attacks their doctrine. He is, however, more 'concerned with determinism as a philosophical thesis in itself' and not so much with a presentation of 'the Stoic system as a whole'. Alexander's presentation of determinism also includes statements that the Stoics would never have accepted, though they could be inferred from their views. Therefore, it 'must be used with considerable caution as evidence' for the reconstruction of the Stoic position.[21] It gives, however, a clear and coherent presentation of a fully deterministic worldview, making it an obvious target for criticism.

Alexander's treatise had a great reputation in the Neoplatonic School. Plotinus studied it, as did probably Proclus himself. It is not impossible that Theodore found here some inspiration in his own attempt to defend a coherent deterministic position.

Alexander composed also a treatise *On Providence*, in which he defended Aristotle's doctrine on providence against the Platonic critique that the philosopher had restricted the activity of providence to the celestial spheres. Alexander admits that divine providence reaches as far as the earth. He does, however, deny that the divine providence takes cares of all small details in this world. The later Platonists continued to criticize the Aristotelians for those erroneous views on providence.[22]

5. The Chaldean Oracles

Another reason for the enduring popularity of the discussion of fate and providence in the imperial period is the growing feeling of many people that they are, as it were, imprisoned in this physical world, subordinated to the celestial powers of stars and planets. This astrological determinism was widespread. Esoteric religious revelations (such as the different forms of Gnosticism) promised the elected to escape from fate. The Chaldean Oracles offer another example of this obsession with fate. In the Oracles the realm of Fate is identical with that of Nature, the lowest part of the World Soul. The personification of Fate is the three-faced goddess Hecate, who, with the demonic powers subordinated to her, exercises authority over the physical world and therefore also plays an important role in magical and theurgical prayers and practices. 'Hecate, princess of the demons, commands the dark powers which enslave the corporeal existence of man, and extends her dominion over all natures, which their fear of the demons had given up to her.'[23]

6. Plotinus

Among the first works of Plotinus is a treatise on Fate, *Ennead* III 1 [3]. In this early work, Plotinus discusses, from a Platonic point of view, the different views on fate defended by Peripatetics, Epicureans, Stoics and astrologers. In his own answer, Plotinus attempts to reconcile a causal explanation of all events (which 'will leave nothing causeless and will preserve sequence and order') with human responsibility (which 'allows us to be something').[24] Plotinus finds a solution in the Platonic doctrine on the soul, taking the soul (both the soul of the universe as the soul of the individual) as an 'initiating cause'. We can admit that all things happen according to causes, if we include among those causes the souls.

Plotinus also introduces a distinction between the soul without the body (which is absolutely free when it follows right reason) and the soul that is in the body and suffers together with the body. Proclus will adopt this distinction between two states of the soul as one of the fundamental principles for any discussion on fate and freedom (see below, p. 16).

Towards the end of his life, Plotinus wrote a lengthy treatise on providence, which Porphyry, in his thematic edition, divided into two parts and put immediately after the early treatise on Fate: *Ennead* III 2-3 [47-8]. The main focus of this treatise is a defence of divine providence against philosophers who deny providence because of the apparent evil in the world, the Epicureans, but also the Peripatetics (who seem to reduce providence to the celestial sphere). In this question, Plotinus takes sides with the Stoics from whom he adopts many arguments, though reading them from a Platonic non-materialistic perspective. The Stoic context may also explain the emphasis on the *Logos* as a rational forming principle of the universe. Since this universal *Logos* contains the *logoi* of all the individual souls, our individual choices of life are included in one universal order.[25] In this treatise Plotinus again stresses that human agents are self-determining principles and that not everything is predetermined by the universal and celestial causes (see III 2 [47] 10). *Ennead* III 2-3 [47-8] is a very important text on problems of theodicy. It is, however, less relevant for the discussion on determinism and free choice.

Finally, there is the important treatise VI 8 [39], wherein Plotinus discusses whether we can also attribute free choice to the gods. As we shall see, Proclus had not much sympathy for these provocative speculations 'on the will of the One'.

7. Porphyry

Porphyry composed a treatise 'On what depends on us', which has been preserved by Stobaeus.[26] The starting point of the discussion is again the myth of Er. Porphyry defends Plato against interpreters who accuse him of undermining free choice in this myth. Before entering the body, every soul can freely choose between different types of life. But once incarnated in a particular body, the free choice of the soul is limited and determined by the particular constitution of the body corresponding to its initial choice. For that reason, fate is not an absolute necessity, but a conditional law. In Porphyry's view Plato composed his myth to react against the astrological beliefs of the Egyptians, according to which the horoscope of our birth determines our choice of life. In the Platonic view, horoscopes only indicate types of life, but do not force them upon the souls.

Porphyry is also the author of the *Sententiae*, which offers a much-read systematic exposition of the doctrine of the *Enneads*. Proclus' reference in this treatise to Porphyry's view on theoretical virtues (see 3,5) is probably a reference to the celebrated discussion of the hierarchy of virtues in chapter 32 of the *Sententiae*.[27]

8. Iamblichus

Among his main sources Proclus mentions 'Iamblichus' innumerable arguments on fate and providence' (*De Prov.* 5,2-3). Of those arguments, we have, alas, only some sections from his letters to Sopater and Macedonius, preserved in the anthology of Stobaeus.[28] The excerpts allow us to understand what Proclus appreciated in Iamblichus, in particular his views on the subordination of fate to providence:

> In its very substance, fate is enmeshed with providence and exists by virtue of the existence of providence, and derives its existence from it and within its ambit.[29]

Iamblichus also insisted on the transcendence of the rational soul beyond the range of fate:

> Insofar as the soul gives itself to the realm of generation and subjects itself to the flow of the universe, thus far also it is drawn beneath the sway of fate and is enslaved to the necessity of nature; but, on the other hand, insofar as it exercises its intellectual activity – activity that is really left free from everything and independent in its choices – thus far it voluntarily 'minds its own business' and lays hold of what is divine and good and intelligible with the accomplishment of truth.[30]

Iamblichus defends providence against the accusations of an unfair distribution of goods contrary to merits. In the fragment from the letter to Sopater, he places the essence of fate in nature, the principle of life and movement, inseparable from the bodies. As we shall see, Proclus concurs with Iamblichus in all these issues.

9. Hierocles

In the early fifth century, Hierocles composed in Alexandria a treatise *On Providence*. We know the content of this treatise only through excerpts and summaries Photius made of it in his *Bibliotheca*.[31] Hierocles understands providence as the order of the universe that proceeds from the divine demiurge. In this providence the gods, the superior beings, as angels and demons, all have their role. Fate is defined as 'the justice that accompanies providence and is subordinated to it'. In the material world providence only reaches as far as genera and species. In order to reconcile free will and fate Hierocles applies the theory of conditional fate, which was developed in Middle Platonism. On many other aspects Hierocles seems to defend positions that remind us of the debate in the Platonic schools of the second and third century. As Photius informs us, Hierocles attacked in his treatise not only the traditional opponents of the Platonists, the Epicureans and the Stoics, but also those who did not interpret the views of Plato and Aristotle correctly. In fact, it is his intention to show that Plato and Aristotle are in fundamental harmony on all important issues. In his own interpretation he follows the line of Ammonius, the teacher of Plotinus in Alexandria, and the whole Platonic tradition, in which he was initiated in Athens through Plutarch, the teacher of Syrianus.

Hierocles was indeed a student of Plutarch in the early fifth century. In the treatise *On Providence* we find the doctrine on providence and fate as it was taught in the Academy in Athens before Syrianus became head of the school and gave it a distinctive direction.

III. Theodore's problems and Proclus' answers

1. General outline of Theodore's worldview

At the beginning of his reply Proclus gives a general outline of the worldview of Theodore:

> Considering the *mise en scène* of human affairs in all sorts of ways, tragic and comic, you believed that the one maker and producer of all those scenes resides solely in the universe, and you called this cause 'fate' (*heimarmenê*); or rather, taking 'fate' to be the connection (*heirmos*) itself of those scenes and the ordered sequence of events, you supposed that this dramaturgy is directed merely by some kind of unalterable necessity; and the latter you celebrate as providence, considering it the only self-determining power (*autexousion*) and mistress of all things, whereas the self-determination of the human soul, about which there is so much talk, is in your opinion only a name and nothing in reality. For the soul is situated in the world and subservient to the actions of other things and is a part of the functioning of the cosmos. Rather, to use your own words, the inescapable cause, which moves all things that this cosmos comprehends within itself, is 'mechanic', and the universe is, as it were, one machine, wherein the celestial spheres are analogous to the interlocking wheels and the particular beings, the animals and the souls, are like the things moved by the wheels, and everything depends upon one moving principle.

As is clear from Proclus' summary, Theodore expressed his deterministic world-view in a vocabulary and with metaphors taken from the Stoic tradition. His claim, however, that human beings have no self-determination goes against Stoic philosophy, though the opponents of the Stoics accused them of making self-determination just a 'name'.

In the Stoic view, all events in the universe 'come to be in accordance with a certain order and sequence'. What in traditional religious language was called *heimarmenê* is understood as the 'inevitable necessity', the 'chain of causes', and the inescapable and unalterable interconnection of all events: 'sempiterna quaedam et indeclinabilis series rerum et catena'.[32] Alexander articulates this deterministic worldview in the following way:

> They say that this universe [...] has an eternal organisation according to a certain sequence and order (*kata heirmon tina kai*

taxin); the things which come to be first are causes for those after them, and in this way all things are bound together with one another. Nothing comes to be in the universe in such a way that there is not something else that follows it with no alternative and is attached to it as to a cause, nor, on the other hand, can any of the things which come to be subsequently be disconnected from the things which have come to be previously, so as not to follow some one of them as if bound to it. But everything which has come to be is followed by something else which of necessity depends on it as a cause, and everything which comes to be has something preceding it to which it is connected as a cause.[33]

We recognise in Proclus' presentation of Theodore's deterministic worldview important elements of this Stoic understanding of fate.

(1) Theodore understands *heimarmenê* as an *heirmos*, a chain interconnecting all events with unalterable necessity.[34] He speaks of a 'necessitas ineuitabilis' (l. 8) and 'causa irrefragabilis' (l. 14), which expressions probably correspond to the Greek *anankê aparabatos* and *aitia anapodrastos*. Both expressions are used in a Stoic context to characterise the necessity of fate. Thus, again, Alexander, *De Fato* 2, p. 166,2-3: 'they understand by fate some cause that is unalterable and inescapable (*aparabaton kai anapodraston*)'.[35]

In the chain of causes the effect follows by necessity upon a preceding cause, and it is itself, in its turn, cause of what follows. For this ordered sequence of events the Stoics used the term *akolouthia* with its double connotation of logical sequence and physical sequence. Theodore uses similar terms: 2,6-7 'consequentem (*akolouthon*) generationem conductam fatum ponens'; 3,4-5 'connexam consequentiam'.

Another expression with Stoic flavour is the verb 'to serve' (*douleuein*) used to indicate the contribution of the parts to the functioning of the whole. Thus Plotinus, in his treatise *On Fate*, characterises the Stoic view:

> [Some call fate] the mutual interweaving of causes and the chain of causation which reaches down from above, and the fact that consequents always follow antecedents and go back to them, since they come to be because of them, and would not have done so without them, and say that what comes after is always enslaved (*douleuein*) to what is before.[36]

(2) In the Stoic view, Fate is identical with Providence, because the divine *Logos* is the ultimate explanation of the interconnection of all causes. This *Logos* is not a transcendent principle, but a force present in the world. This is also Theodore's opinion, as Proclus writes: 'you believed that the one maker and producer of all those scenes resides solely in the universe, and you called this cause fate'. Yet Theodore makes a conceptual distinction between providence and fate, as Proclus further explains:

> Providence and fate are not to be distinguished as you formulate it in your letter, making the latter the connected sequence [of events], the former the necessity causing this [sequence].[37]

For Proclus, this distinction is inadequate. If providence is an immanent cause within the world, it cannot be really distinguished from fate. In his Platonic understanding even fate keeps some transcendence *vis-à-vis* what is fated.

(3) Theodore compares the connection of events in the universe with the organisation of a drama, it may be comical or tragic, and wherein its producer connects the different scenes: 'rerum humanarum omnimodas tragicas et comicas aliasve funes'. The metaphor of the theatre was very popular in the imperial philosophical schools in the discussions of providence and fate. It was used by Cynics, Stoics, Peripatetics, and by the Platonists themselves. Cicero (following Chrysippus) talks of the world as 'quemadmodum theatrum', Epictetus reminds us that we are the actors of a drama we have not composed ourselves, and Marcus Aurelius speaks in the same sense.[38] Even Alexander talks about fate as a drama.[39] Plotinus exploits the image with brio in his treatise *On Providence*, exploiting much Stoic material.[40] Proclus adapts the same image in this reply to Theodore in ch. 34,26-30 below: 'for every human deed is a part of the universe, but not vice versa. For also the other living beings, which are parts of the universe, must do something but also undergo something. And every part of this cosmic system and drama has the good as its end'. Moreover, he develops the metaphor at length in *De Decem Dub.* 60,18-22. 'For in our lives the whole period of a tribe is analogous to a drama, fate to the producer of this drama, the souls to the persons contributing to the drama: sometimes different souls, sometimes the same souls playing [different roles on] this fatale scene. Similarly on the theatre the same actors speak sometimes for Teiresias, sometimes for Oedipus.'

(4) The fact that Theodore understands the world as a connection of dramatic scenes could not be seen as provocative. It is a common opinion among almost all philosophers in late antiquity, including Christian thinkers. What Proclus, however, could never accept is Theodore's explanation of the world as a complex mechanical clock, whereby the celestial spheres function as the wheels setting into movement all the beings inside the mechanism, living as well as not living. This mechanistic metaphor is not of Stoic provenance. For the Stoics understood the world rather in organic terms, as a great living being wherein all things and events are connected through *sympatheia* and *sympnoia*. The terminology used by Theodore seems to come from astronomical sources. One is also reminded of the mechanical explanation the Epicureans offered of the functioning of the world: forces using levers, wheels and bars. In Cicero, *On the Nature of the Gods* 1.19, an Epicurean philosopher criticises Plato for having failed to explain the mechanism of the creation of the world: 'quae molitio, quae machinae, qui ministri tanti numeris fuerunt'. The Platonists always ridiculed this simplistic understanding of causality.[41] And at the end of his treatise, Proclus again uses the metaphor of a mechanical clock as an *ad hominem* argument against Theodore. Even Theodore has to admit that the astronomer, before producing an astronomical clock made with wheels and rotating pin, must have in his mind an intellectual, incorporeal paradigm of what he wants to produce.[42] *A fortiori* the structure of the world must exist in the mind of the divine creator before being made in corporeal structures.

(5) Seeing the world as a mechanical clock, which determines everything with unalterable necessity, Theodore can conclude that the 'self-determination (*autexousion*) of the human soul', about which philosophers like to talk so much, is only a name, but nothing in reality. Only divine providence (identified with fate) can be considered as a free power, since it has sovereignty over all things, whereas all things inside the system, including the human souls, are subservient to it. This conclusion is definitely not Stoic. As we have seen, the Stoics always emphatically defended the compatibility of determinism and free choice.[43] Even if all external things are necessitated, it remains in our power how we react to what happens. Their opponents, however, insisted that their radical determinism left no room for human responsibility. How is it possible, Alexander asked in his treatise *On Fate*, if all things happen in accordance with fate, to preserve not just the name of 'what depends on us' but also the common conception we have of this notion, namely that choice really matters? It seems that the Stoics with all their insistence on 'what depends on us' only kept the name (*onoma monon*).[44] Plotinus, in his own treatise *On Fate*, repeats the same critique: 'what depends on us will only be a name'.[45] It cannot be a simple coincidence that Theodore uses the same phrase, not, however, to criticise the Stoics, but to ridicule all philosophers who defend the possibility of free choice. In a deterministic universe there can be no room for such a human faculty, the only free power being that of the despotic fate or providence itself.

(6) Although Theodore uses no explicit astrological arguments in his letter to Proclus, the fact that he understands the whole world as a mechanical system is a sufficient proof that he probably adhered to a form of astrological determinism, which was very popular among pagan intellectuals in the last centuries of the Roman empire.

The most impressive document on the dominance of astrological determinism among pagan intellectuals in the fourth century is the vast treatise on astrology, *Mathesis*, composed by the Roman senator Julius Firmicus Maternus between 334 and 337. Although this author is influenced by Platonic views (in particular in his notion of the supreme

Introduction

God), he attacks Plotinus because 'he attributes nothing to the power of the stars and reserves nothing for the necessity of fate, but says that everything is in our power' ('totum dicens in nostra esse positum potestate'). He also criticises those who accept that birth and death are 'sub fato', but maintain that 'the course of our life (*cursum uitae*) is in our power'. But, if the 'necessity of fatal laws' determine the beginning and end of our life, how could what is between those terms escape fate?[46]

There is, of course, no influence of this Latin author on Theodore, but it is interesting to see in Firmicus' case a similar attitude: a pagan author with sympathies for Neoplatonism, but defending a deterministic view.

In this context, it is also worth referring to the short treatise *Against Fate* that Gregory of Nyssa composed at the end of the fourth century. As Gregory explains, this treatise is the refutation of a number of arguments that a pagan philosopher had put forward in favour of determinism during a debate in Constantinople (maybe in 381 at the time of the church council ... if the public dispute is not a literary *topos*!). Proclus never read Christian texts and was not influenced by their arguments.[47] Yet, it is interesting to notice that the pagan philosopher with whom Gregory had a discussion defended a radical determinism similar to that of Theodore.[48]

2. Three preliminary distinctions

The main focus of Proclus' treatise is to solve the various problems that Theodore put forward regarding the hypothesis of free choice. This is done in the second part of the treatise (chs 33-66). Before, however, entering the discussion of each of the eight problems Proclus discusses in a first general part (chs 3-32) three distinctions, which, in his view, are fundamental presuppositions in the whole debate. For if the opponents do not agree on these three points, it is useless to go on with the discussion.

> It is my view that, if you want to track down the problems under investigation, you should above all examine the following three distinctions. *First* is the distinction between providence and fate [...]. The *second* distinction is that between two types of soul. The one is separable from the body [...] the other is that which resides in the bodies and is inseparable from its substrates. The latter depends in its being upon fate, the former upon providence. The *third* distinction concerns knowledge and truth. One type [of knowledge] exists in souls that are engaged in the process of generation; [...] another type is present in souls that have escaped from this place [...]. If you sufficiently grasp the three distinctions we mentioned, the solution to all the problems you raised will become clear.[49]

As Proclus explains, these distinctions were all made in the Platonic tradition before him. In fact, as we shall see, the distinctions are traditional and go back to Middle Platonism and even to Plato himself 'if one is capable of following him'.

(a) The distinction between providence and fate
Providence and fate are both causes of what happens in this world, but not in the same order. Providence precedes fate, fate is subordinated to it. All things that happen according to fate happen also according to providence. The converse, however, is not true. For the rational souls and the superior classes (such as angels) are not subjected to fate, though they cannot escape providence. Fate only governs physical events, bodies and bodily qualities, whereas providence encompasses both what is corporeal and incorporeal.

Proclus credits Iamblichus 'in his numerous writings on providence and fate' with this distinction. But as we have seen, it is a commonplace in discussions in Middle Platonism.

(b) The distinction between separable and inseparable souls
We have to distinguish with Plato between two types of souls: the rational soul, which is separable from body, and the irrational, which is inseparable from a bodily substrate. Whereas the latter is subservient to necessity, the former transcends fate. Also Aristotle made this distinction a fundamental principle of his doctrine of the soul.[50]

All Platonic philosophers, Proclus says, make use of this distinction in their defence of free choice. Thus Plotinus in III 1 [3] 8,9-15:

> When the soul is without body it is in absolute control of itself and free, and outside the causation of the physical universe; but when it is brought onto body it is no longer in all ways in control, as it forms part of an order of other things. [...] But sometimes it masters them itself and leads them where it wishes. The better soul has power over more, the worse over less.

As we have seen, Iamblichus also defended this view (see above, p. 10).

(c) Different modes of knowledge
The third preamble distinction concerns the different ways of obtaining knowledge of the truth. On the one hand, there is knowledge that souls may acquire when engaged in this world of becoming, on the other hand, knowledge that is present in the souls when they have escaped from this body and have been established in the intelligible realm. Proclus distinguishes five levels of knowledge: (1) opinion, (2) mathematical science, (3) dialectical science, (4) intellect, and (5) a union with the divine beyond knowledge.[51] The relevance of these epistemological distinctions for the discussion of freedom may be less evident. However, as we shall

Introduction

see, Theodore not only raised problems on free choice, but also had doubts whether we could ever obtain true knowledge on this issue. Following Plotinus and Porphyry, Proclus defends that it is possible for the soul, even during this earthly life, to reach intellectual contemplation and even a state of union with the divine. When someone actualises this most divine activity of the soul, 'he will become a god as far as this is possible for a soul, and will know in the way the gods know everything in an ineffable manner'.

3. Theodore's eight problems

Having examined these three fundamental distinctions, which are necessary presuppositions in any philosophical discussion on fate and providence, Proclus finally turns to the different problems Theodore had raised in his letter and addresses each of them separately.

(a) Refusal of responsibility for failures
'We consider ourselves responsible for the outcome, whenever we do the right thing, but whenever we fail, we transfer the responsibility to necessity rather than to our choice' (ch. 33). Theodore concludes from this fact that we all believe that the universe is a deterministic system where there is no room for free choice.

That people only claim responsibility for what goes right, and reject it for what goes wrong, is a common human predicament. In the celebrated myth of Er, Plato lets the soul that makes a wrong choice, complain:

> When he inspected his fate, he beat his breast and bewailed his choice. [...] he did not blame himself for his woes, but fortune and the gods and anything except himself.[52]

Yet, the prophet had warned the souls that 'responsibility is with him who chooses, not with god' (*Resp.* 617E). Similarly, in the *Laws*, the Athenian criticises the behaviour of someone who thinks that 'responsibility for his faults lies not in himself, but in others, whom he blames for his most frequent and serious misfortunes, while exonerating himself'.[53] This attitude was also sharply criticised by the Stoics. In his *Enchiridion*, Epictetus says:

> It is the part of the uneducated person to blame others where he himself is not doing well; to blame himself is the part of one whose education has begun; to blame neither oneself nor another is the part of one whose education is already complete.[54]

Proclus fully endorses this view, as is clear from the following passage from his commentary on the *Alcibiades*:

> The Stoics are accustomed to say, and rightly too, that the uneducated man blames others, and not himself, for his own misfortune; but the person who makes progress attributes to himself the responsibility for all his evil words and deeds, while the educated man blames neither himself nor others.[55]

Proclus finds an example of this wrong moral attitude in the young Alcibiades, who blamed Socrates, and not himself, for his ignorance. Socrates then is right when he rebukes him: 'you accuse me in vain'.[56]

To conclude, Theodore is right in his observation that many people blame fate for what goes wrong. This is, however, characteristic of immoral non-educated people. The virtuous person will not show such behaviour. Therefore, Theodore is wrong in making this an argument against free choice.

(b) The argument from divination
'Human beings are always curious to know about the future, even in matters that seem to depend on us. This is shown by our interest in divination even in matters where we ourselves make a choice'. Hence, Theodore concludes, 'if we are all lovers of divination, nothing depends on us' (ch. 37).

The practice and alleged success of divination was one of the standard arguments of the Stoics for the determinism of the universe. In his *On Fate*, Chrysippus presented the following argument: 'The predictions of the soothsayers could not be true, if all things were not embraced by fate'.[57] Such an argument is also developed in Cicero's *On Divination*.[58] In his attack on determinism, Alexander mentions this Stoic position: 'those who sing the praises of prophecy and say that it is preserved only by their own [deterministic] account, and use it as a proof that all things come to be in accordance with fate'.[59] Similarly Calcidius: 'they say that divination clearly demonstrates that the outcome is already determined by fate (*prouentus iam dudum esse decretos*)'.[60] Against this position one may object, as Alexander writes, that it renders prophecy useless or makes it a determining factor in the outcome of the predicted awful events, what means that we have to make the gods themselves responsible for the evil done by Oedipus. The Middle Platonists used the example of oracles to show that what they predict is not absolutely necessary, but depends on how people react to oracles: they only express a conditional fate (see above, p. 6). Proclus' answer stands in the same tradition.

(c) One vital force permeating the universe
Although the beginning of chapter 39 betrays a lacuna, it is not too difficult to reconstruct Theodore's argument from the context and the subsequent criticism of Proclus. Theodore believes that one and the same vital force governs the whole universe. It penetrates all beings and

gives life, in a descending scale, according to the different capacities of the receiving bodies. In the human brains this vital force is the rational soul, in the sense organs it is the sensitive life, which again is differentiated according to the diverse organs wherein it is incarnated. The origin of this cosmic vital force is situated in the ether. Even the divine soul governing the whole universe is made of this ether.

Here again Theodore may have been influenced by his reading of some handbook on Stoicism. In the physical theory of the Stoics, the universe and all the beings it contains result from the activity of the *Logos* pervading the whole universe and acting upon matter. This *Logos* is not an immaterial principle, but performs its creative function as a breath (*pneuma*), a full blending of fire and air, that maintains all things in being. According to the different degrees of this 'containment', different types of beings come to exist: rational beings, living organisms, plants, bones and sinews. In some texts, however, the ether itself is considered to be the ruling principle. Thus, in the summary of Stoic physics in Diogenes Laertius:

> The whole world is a living being, endowed with soul and reason, and having ether for its ruling principle: so says Antipater of Tyre [...]; and Chrysippus says that it is the purer part of ether; the same which they declare to be the primary god and always to have, as it were in a sensible manner, pervaded all that is in the air, all animals and plants, and also the earth itself, as principle of cohesion.[61]

Although the Stoics did not consider the ether a 'fifth element', in the later schools their doctrine of the divine *Logos-pneuma*, which permeates the world, could easily be conflated with the view of the soul as entelechy of the ethereal body, which was defended by some Aristotelians.[62] In Platonic adaptations of the Stoic doctrine, the ruling principle of the world is often considered a 'soul permeating the world', from which 'all consequent causes are brought into action in a continuous interweaving, called fate'.[63]

In this context one may understand why Theodore speaks of an ethereal soul descending from the highest sphere of the universe into all levels of beings, becoming reason, the different sense perceptions and vegetative life. On one point, however, Theodore diverges from the Stoics. For the Stoics it was not the brain, but the heart that was the central organ of the rational life: a thesis often attacked by the Platonists, and most notoriously by Galen.[64] On this point, then, the eclectic Theodore reveals his Platonic sympathies.

(d) Intermezzo: hedonism
Theodore next claims that 'the good is what is pleasurable to each individual, and that it is so by convention: for different customs prevail among different people (ch. 45).

We have here a stock argument in favour of hedonism and relativism. This hedonism does not come from the Epicurean tradition. The argument resembles rather the position of the hedonists Plato introduces in the *Gorgias* and in the *Philebus*. In particular, the opposition between 'by nature' (*phusei*) and 'by convention' (*thesei*) seems to point in this direction. Plato, however, never uses *thesei* in this context, but *nomôi* or *technêi*. The opposition *phusei-thesei* is characteristic for the discussion in the Hellenistic schools, in particular in the debate on the natural or conventional character of names.[65]

One may wonder why Theodore introduces this argument in a discussion about free choice. Proclus explains that this hedonistic position follows from the preceding erroneous view. Once the soul is considered to be a material principle, it is no longer possible to distinguish between what is pleasurable (i.e. good for the senses) and what is absolutely good.

> But, as it appears, it was true that 'given one absurdity, others follow.' This is what happens to you, I believe. For having made fate superior to soul, you have ranked the soul together with the irrational perceptions; and having concluded that they are the same thing, you have made the good and the pleasurable one (ch. 46).

It may be, however, that Theodore had other reasons to defend this relativistic hedonism. If everything is determined and if whatever we do follows from previous conditions, it is vain to search for an end of life transcending the material conditions of our existence. If we can never know what the objective good may be (see the next argument), let us enjoy our life as much as possible! This is the only message a deterministic and sceptical philosopher may give.

One should also notice that the diversity of customs among different nations (the so-called *nomima barbarika*) was a stock argument against astrological determinism since Carneades. If the precise horoscope at the moment of birth determines the physical constitution, character and mode of life of every individual, how can we explain that individuals born under quite different constellations share as a group (tribe, nation), the same traditional customs and even the same physique?[66] The defenders of astrology attempted to refute this argument, insisting for example on various forms of geographical determinism (where the constellations may explain common features of some nations). It is not impossible that Theodore is influenced by this tradition when he points to the different customs prevailing among different people.

(e) Scepticism
This is without doubt the most interesting section in Theodore's letter to Proclus. Exploiting passages from Plato's dialogues, Theodore defends a sceptical position, which claims that the truth cannot be known,

adducing Socrates as his philosophical example (ch. 48). Four arguments can be distinguished:

(1) Socrates often says that 'he knows nothing' and he ridicules those who pretend to know all things. There is the celebrated passage in the *Apology* wherein Socrates explains the meaning of the oracle. He is 'the wisest' of all Greeks, because he is the only one who knows that he does not know (*Apol.* 20E-23B). In many dialogues we find Socrates defending the same position. See, for instance, *Symp.* 216D, *Theaet.* 150C, *Resp.* 1, 337E, *Meno* 80A. In the *Apology*, he explains that he has become unpopular by 'disproving the claim of wisdom' of those who pretend to know. The same ridicule of people that claim to know all things can be found in *Sophist* 232E-234C.

(2) Socrates declares in the *Phaedo* (66D-68A) that the soul will only know the full truth after it becomes dissociated from the earthly body. 'If we are ever to have pure knowledge, we must escape from the body.' Socrates therefore has 'good hope' that 'on arriving where he is going, he will acquire what has been our chief preoccupation in this past life.' This conviction, however, disproves that one can reach a perfect knowledge in this world.

(3) In the *Republic*, Socrates establishes that even the most accurate sciences, i.e. mathematical sciences, when compared with dialectic, are not really sciences, because they cannot give an account of their own suppositions (cf. *Resp.* 7, 533B6-C5).

(4) And finally, in the same context Socrates uses the verb 'to dream' (*oneirôttein*) to characterise the scientific activities: 'they dream about what is, they are unable to hold a waking view as long as they use hypotheses' (*Resp.* 7, 533B8-C2; cf. 534C8). From an earlier passage in the dialogue we know that Socrates uses the metaphor of the 'dreaming' rather pejoratively to refer to those who live in an illusionary world of the senses without being capable to see the forms (cf. *Resp.* 5, 476C5-8; cf. also *Theaet.* 158B3).

The arguments of Theodore are not new. The philosophers who defended in the New Academy a sceptical interpretation of Plato used them all to demonstrate that there is no doctrine in Plato's dialogues, only a discussion of problems. Commenting on the passage from the *Theaetetus* (150C4) where Socrates declares that he knows nothing, the anonymous commentator writes: 'Starting from this and similar passages some consider Plato as an 'academic philosopher', since he defends no doctrine (*ouden dogmatizonta*)'.[67] The strongest argument for a Platonic scepticism was, of course, the fact that Socrates often admitted his ignorance. Thus, Arcesilas, who defended the view that nothing can be known, insisted that even the knowledge Socrates had left for himself, namely the fact that he knows that he does not know, cannot be known.[68]

From the first century onwards, the dogmatic interpretation of Plato prevailed in the schools. Neoplatonic philosophy is the most perfect expression of this dogmatic form of Platonism. It is surprising, then, to find again a defence of a sceptical reading of Plato at the end of ancient philosophy. That may be taken as another proof that the sceptical tendency never really disappeared in Platonism.[69] We find a confirmation of the persistence of scepticism in later Platonism in Proclus' *Commentary on Euclid*. In his introduction, Proclus informs us that, even in the Platonic school, some philosophers denied the utility of the study of the mathematical sciences, referring to Plato's arguments on the mathematics in *Republic* V. It is remarkable to find the engineer Theodore in that company. Against those critics within the school Proclus adduces other arguments from Plato, which demonstrate how important the mathematical training is for philosophers and he offers a different interpretation of the argument in the *Republic*.[70]

In the same manner Proclus refutes, in this reply to Theodore, all arguments that seek to make Socrates a sceptical philosopher. In any case, Theodore is foolish when he believes that his scepticism could ever be a convincing argument for a deterministic worldview. 'If it is not possible to know the truth, we also do not know whether there is something that depends on us or not'.[71] For scepticism only allows for agnostic positions.

(f) Misfortune of good people
'Next you formulate the following problem: why do the good fare badly, failing to achieve the goals they have set, whereas the bad achieve what they desire' (ch. 53).

This is indeed, as Proclus says, one of the most common arguments against providence. It is so traditional that Sextus Empiricus, in his *Outlines of Pyrrhonism*, can use it as an example of opposing philosophical views: 'When someone establishes the existence of providence from the order of the heavenly bodies, we oppose to this the fact that often the good fare badly (*duspragein*) and the bad prosper (*eupragein*), and conclude from this that providence does not exist'.[72] The same argument against providence is used by the Academic Cotta in Cicero's *On the Nature of the Gods*, 3.79. But already Plato criticised traditional poetry for voicing this complaint: 'they say that the gods assign misfortune and a bad life to good people, and the opposite fate to their opposites' (*Resp.* 2, 364B). The Neoplatonists refuted the objection with the Stoic argument that 'a good person can never suffer any evil'. In his discussion of *Ten Problems on Providence and Fate*, Proclus devotes the sixth question entirely to this issue.[73] As Proclus declares here, this argument fits better in a discussion on providence than in a debate of free choice:

> to my knowledge, none of the ancient philosophers has put forward this problem in order to eliminate that which depends on us, but rather to examine providence. The famous Plotinus, Iamblichus and your namesake [sc. Theodore of Asine] have relentlessly struggled with this problem.

(g) Real freedom is a divine privilege

Theodore next raises a question, which, as Proclus observes, he had better put at the beginning of his arguments. He examines the meaning of the expression 'what depends us' (*eph' hêmin*) and defines it as 'that which is by nothing dominated or mastered, but is self-determined (*autoperigraptos*) and self-activated (*autoenergêtos*)'. He concludes that only the divinity, 'the first lord of all beings', can have this absolute power of self-determination, whereas we humans are deprived of it.

Theodore characterises 'what depends on us' as *autoperigrapton* and *auto-energêton*. The latter term is not infrequent in later Neoplatonism, and in particular in Proclus, who often uses it with regard of the soul. As a self-moving principle, the soul is not just acted upon, but is always also self-activating, as is clear in the process of knowledge. See *in Alc.* 248,15-17; 279,25-7; *in Eucl.* 15,26ff. and in this treatise, *De Prov.* 44,16. The second term is nowhere else attested. Damascius, however, uses the term *autoperigraphos* nine times, in the sense of 'what circumscribes or contains one self', and this usage is particular to him alone.[74] Since Theodore understands 'what depends on us' as absolute self-determination, he can only admit that 'the first Ruler of all things', which is in his view divine Fate,[75] can have such a power.

Proclus replies that Theodore takes the expression 'what depends on us' in a sense that deviates from the traditional understanding. For the ancient philosophers never understood the expression *eph' hêmin* as absolute freedom or licence or self-determination, but used it to indicate our faculty of choice. This faculty does not make us master of everything we would want to happen or not, but makes us, through our preferences, responsible for our actions. This free choice between what is good and is not is to be distinguished from the will, which only aims at the good. The gods exercise their will, but do not have the faculty of choice between alternatives. Therefore, what is *eph' hêmin* is characteristic of human action, not divine, as Theodore believes.

Already Plotinus raised the question whether we may apply the notion *eph' hêmin* to divine agents and to the One itself:

> First we must ask what something 'depending on us' ought to mean; that is, what is the notion of such a thing; for in this way it might come to be known whether it is suitable to transfer it to the gods and, still more, to God, or whether it should not be transferred.[76]

Plotinus defended the use of the term in the case of the gods who have absolute freedom: everything is in their power. Proclus, however, returns to the traditional Stoic notion of *eph' hêmin*, limiting it to human agency, and carefully distinguishes it from the notion of 'will' and 'voluntary' (*hekousion*). This is also the view defended by Simplicius in his commentary on Epictetus: the faculty of choice is situated solely in the human rational soul, which holds an ambivalent position between the inferior and the superior.[77]

(h) Colophon: divine providence excludes human freedom
Finally, Theodore asks whether god knows what will happen to us or not. If he does not know it, he will not be different from us who do not know it either. But if he knows it, whatever he knows will absolutely and by necessity happen. This, however not only removes that which depends on us, but also whatever is called contingent (ch. 62).

This is, as Proclus says, an argument 'that has been formulated a thousand times': 'if god knows whatever will be, what will be will happen of necessity'.[78] It is indeed one of the standard arguments of all determinists, as Alexander informs us:

> Assuming that the gods have foreknowledge of the things that are going to be they establish that they come to be of necessity, on the grounds that, if they did not come to be in this way, [the gods] would not have foreknowledge of them.[79]

As Alexander shows, such a view removes all contingency from the world, and hence the possibility of that which depends on us. Even philosophers, who do not admit full determinism, but grant that there is real contingency in this world, will be forced to acknowledge 'that all things are necessitated', if they accept that there is divine foreknowledge. Therefore, the Aristotelians limited providence to the superlunary realm.

Proclus had already discussed this problem extensively in the second of the *Ten Questions about Providence*. His answer to Theodore is nothing but an application of the views he had expressed before. Both here and in that treatise Proclus attempts to reconcile the opposing views of the Stoics (who, in order to save providence, abolish contingency and reduce everything to necessity) and the Peripatetics (who, in order to save contingency, restrict providence to the celestial spheres).

> Let us examine in what sense we may say that providence knows contingent things, as also the ancients have set out the depth of this problem thoroughly. Because of this problem, some philosophers, who acknowledge providence, have removed the nature of the contingent from among beings, whereas others, who admit that the evidence of the contingent cannot be contested, deny that providence reaches down to that level.[80]

The Peripatetics also maintained that the divine foreknowledge of the future contingent could only be indeterminate lest the future events themselves become necessitated. For a determinate knowledge is only possible of determinate events. As Alexander argues:

He who has foreknowledge of the things that are contingent will have foreknowledge of them *as such*. [...] So the gods too would have foreknowledge of the things that are contingent *as contingent*, and necessity will not at all follow on this, on account of foreknowledge of *this* sort.[81]

Against this Peripatetic view Proclus argues that the gods can have a *determinate* and certain knowledge of indeterminate and uncertain future events.

Every god has an undivided knowledge of things divided and a timeless knowledge of things temporal; he knows the contingent without contingency, the mutable immutably.[82]

Proclus' solution is based on a principle that was first formulated by Iamblichus, as can be inferred from Ammonius' commentary on *De Interpretatione* (136,14ff.). We should not characterise the modes of knowing by the nature of the objects known (as Porphyry had argued, defending as Alexander that the gods know what is indeterminate as indeterminate). It is the opposite: 'the manner of knowing becomes different through the differences in the knowers': 'secundum cognoscentis proprietatem et cognitio determinata est'.[83] Knowledge must not have the character of the object known, but of the knowing subject. Therefore, the gods will know the corporeal and temporal things in a superior way.

4. Conclusion

In this treatise Proclus offers a solution of Theodore's problems and his arguments in favour of radical determinism. But, as Proclus observes in his conclusion, he could have developed many more arguments to demonstrate directly that we are capable of free choice. For if we were not responsible of our actions, all human ethical and political education would be in vain. Even philosophy itself would be an idle endeavour if nothing depends on us, as Proclus' teacher Syrianus repeatedly said.

That a deterministic explanation of the universe undermined the intuitions and beliefs of our ethical and political life, was a standard argument in defence of free choice. In his refutation of determinism Alexander devotes five chapters on the unfortunate consequences of determinism for our moral life: praise and blame, reward and punishment, education make no more sense.[84] In the Stoic view, however, moral responsibility was compatible with physical determinism. Even in a deterministic universe it makes sense to praise and punish and educate, as our actions enter the causal chain and thus may contribute to a change of behaviour. Hence Seneca already anticipated Syrianus' question: 'quid mihi prodest philosophia, si fatum est'.[85]

Finally, Proclus encourages Theodore to consider the arguments in favour of free choice again and again. If Theodore is still in doubts, he should not hesitate to write to him again. For one could never accuse a philosopher of engaging in idle talk when discussing arguments with such relevance for practical life! However, Proclus warns Theodore that he should not let himself be carried away by the niceties of the Stoics who, with all their deceitful arguments, want to make us believe that the world is a fully deterministic system.[86] This is a surprising conclusion, because, as we have seen, the position of Theodore is eclectic, and certainly not that of an orthodox Stoic. It seems, however, that Proclus here finally returns to the century-old debate wherein Stoics and Platonists are opposed in the defence of the free will. The questions of Theodore provoked him to attack, from a Platonic view, the Stoic deterministic view of the world, of which Theodore only represents a simplistic version. Therefore, the first general part of this refutation is for Proclus more important than the point by point critique in the second part.

IV. Analysis of the argument

Introduction

[1] Proclus thanks Theodore for having sent him a letter in which he formulates a number of problems concerning free choice, fate and providence. The questions Theodore raises are not new: they have often been discussed in the tradition and will always provoke us to further investigation. In accordance with this tradition and in particular Plato Proclus will offer his own views.

[2] Summary of the deterministic worldview of Theodore.

Part I. Three preliminary distinctions

[3-5a] Before tackling each of the eight problems Proclus discusses three distinctions which, in his view, are fundamental presuppositions in the debate on freedom and determinism: (1) the distinction between fate and providence; (2) the distinction between the separable and inseparable soul; (3) the distinction between different levels of knowledge. Iamblichus is credited for having clarified the first distinction. All Platonists have made the second distinction. Plotinus and Porphyry have often discussed the third.

1. The distinction between providence and fate

[5b] Before one examines what something is one has to examine whether it exists. Since Theodore accepts the existence of providence

and fate, but has erroneous views about both, Proclus can skip the first question and direct his attention to the question 'what providence and fate are'.

[6] In order to discover what providence and fate are two methods are recommended. First we should start from the common notions we all have on providence and fate and clarify and articulate what is confused in them. Second, we have to apply dialectic, which teaches us 'the division of beings according to articulations'. The main divisions within reality are the intelligible realm, the intellectual, the psychic, the corporeal, each having different characters. Once we have discovered what providence and fate truly are (see 7-8), we shall examine on what level of reality each of them can be applied (see 9-14).

[7] The common notions of fate and providence: providence is 'the cause of goods for those governed by it', fate is 'the cause of some connection and sequence between things that occur'. That we have those common notions is demonstrated with examples of how we speak of *pronoein* and *heimarmenê*. Proclus examines not only our ordinary language but also the expert language of the prophets of the Chaldean Oracles.

[8] If providence and fate are causes, they cannot be identical with their effects. In fact, we have to distinguish three elements: (1) the cause (providence, or fate), (2) the activity proceeding from the cause ('to provide' or 'to connect'), (3) the subject of the activity (what is subject to providence, what is subject to fate). If the cause is superior to the effect it produces, providence will be the source of good, without itself being made good, fate the cause of connection, without itself being connected.

[9] After having articulated our common notions of providence and fate, we will investigate, using dialectic, their domains. First we will examine what the 'connected things' are, the domain of fate.
Three ontological levels must be distinguished: (1) some beings have both substance and activity in eternity; (2) some exist in time and have an activity in time; (3) some are intermediary between (1) and (2): they have an eternal substance but a temporal activity. Proclus justifies this threefold division insisting on the necessity of an intermediary and excluding possibility (4): there are no beings with a temporal substance and an eternal activity. The three ontological levels are respectively what is intellectual, what is corporeal and what is psychic.

[10] Where among those three levels should we put 'the things that are interconnected by fate'? Interconnected things are divided, dissociated either in place or time, though capable of being connected by another cause. Hence, they are 'moved by another' and corporeal.

[11] What is the proximate cause of the movements of the bodies? We first take the example of our own body: what is the cause that moves it and nourishes it? Its nature or vegetative power. So also in the whole world there is a single nature of the world maintaining and moving everything in it.

[12] Fate is the nature of this world, an incorporeal substance and life moving and connecting all parts in it, the superior and the inferior.

[13] We now turn to providence. As source of all good it must be a divine cause. For only god is unqualifiedly good. Further, since it presides over both the intelligible and the sensible, it must be superior to fate (which only governs the sensible). Whatever falls under fate, falls under providence, not however, the other way around. Plato expresses the subordination of fate to providence in the *Timaeus* saying that the world is a 'mixture of intellect and necessity whereby the intellect rules over necessity'. 'Necessity' here is synonymous with 'fate'.

[14] Conclusion: there are two realms, the intellectual and the sensible, the former ruled by providence, the latter by fate. Fate is divine insofar as it participates in the divinity, providence is divine *per se* and primary.

2. The distinction between the separable and inseparable soul

[15] The principle at the basis of the distinction is well formulated by Aristotle: 'every soul with an activity that does not need body also has a substance free from body and separable'. Once this general principle is established we should examine what kind of soul could be separable from body. Proclus examines successively five types of soul in order to see if they need bodily organs in their activities.

[16] (1) Sense perception: they need affections in the sense organs, ears, eyes, etc. (2) Appetitive and irascible faculties: the emotions of anger and desire are always accompanied with physical change in bodily organs, heart and liver. Besides, they depend on sense perceptions.

[17] (3) Opinion (*doxa*): here we come already to the level of the rational soul. Opinion passes judgement over the senses and the emotions, which are incapable of reflection on their own activities. This judgement over perception is manifest in the critique of perceptive illusion. Opinion brings also discipline in our emotional life, attempting to contain the desires, drawing back the irascible part from its impulses. This judgement of the opinative faculty occurs, not through bodily organs, but through reflecting inwards and 'looking at its own internal reasons'. In this activity the soul dissociates itself from body.

[18] (4) discursive reasoning (*dianoia*): the soul discovers in itself a 'rational world', image of the intelligible, paradigm of the sensible. This rational activity is expressed in the mathematical sciences, which purify the soul from body.

[19] (5) intellect (*nous*): intuitive knowledge which brings the soul to the level of the gods.

[20] Summary and application on the problem of fate: whenever the rational soul moves according to its nature, it gets outside of body. Hence, it must also have a substance that is separable from body. Therefore, when the soul acts according to its nature, it is superior to fate; but when it is brought down to sense perception and made irrational and corporeal, it is dominated by the cause that reigns over them.

[21] Confirmation by the Chaldean Oracles, which teach us how we can escape fate.

[22] The soul is free when it does not attach itself to the external goods, which fall under the power of others. Illustration by personal experience in Proclus' life.

[23] If we focus on the superior rational activities of the soul, we will admire its freedom, its virtue without master. When we protest and suffer and desire and complain, it is not our true 'we', but something inferior associated to it.

[24] Every soul has as much freedom as it has a share of virtue.

[25] The soul is intermediary between intellect and body. Intellect is always superior to necessity, body always subject to it. The soul can either take side with the former and be free or with the latter and be subservient to necessity.

[26] When you want to see what depends on us, look at a soul that lives in accordance with its nature.

3. Different modes of knowledge

[27] Account of the five different modes of knowledge. *First*, knowledge that only grasps the truth of the fact without its cause (*doxa*).

[28] *Second*, knowledge that proceeds from principles taken as suppositions and draws necessary conclusions: the mathematical reasoning, which is characteristic of *dianoia*.

[29] *Third*, knowledge that ascends through all the forms towards the unconditional principle, using division and analysis (dialectics).

[30] *Fourth*, intuitive knowledge: it no longer uses methods such as analysis or synthesis or division or demonstration, but contemplates beings by means of simple intuitions.

[31] *Fifth*, knowledge beyond the intellect, which is called 'divine madness'; it arouses the 'one of the soul' and connects it with the One itself. For all things are known by something similar to them: the sensible by sense perception, the scientific objects by science, the intelligible Forms by the intellect, the One by what is like the One. Only Platonists admit this superior form of knowledge.

[32] When someone actualises what is the most divine activity of the soul, he will become a god as far as this is possible for a soul, and will know in the way the gods know everything.

Part II. Solution of the problems raised by Theodore
1. Argument: refusal of responsibility for failures

[33] The argument: whenever we are successful, we consider ourselves responsible for the outcome, but whenever we fail, we transfer responsibility to 'fate'.

[34] This is alas common practice among humans. But wise persons do not blame everything on higher powers. As Plato in the *Laws*, they consider god as source of good. The periodic revolution of the world is a second cause in the government of the universe. We ourselves function as a third cause. We are part of the universe and undergo something, but also have our own particular contribution.

[35] We share control over external events with the superior causes; but we are fully master of our interior choices and impulses.

[36] The faculty that depends on us is a capacity of choice. We praise or blame someone because of his choice not because of the outcome of his choices in action.

2. The argument from divination

[37] Argument: all humans are curious to know the future and are therefore fascinated by prophecies and divination. Divination only works if the future is predetermined and can be known. Therefore, if we are lovers of divination, nothing depends on us.

Introduction

Proclus reverses the argument. If nothing depends on us and all events are necessitated, why should we have an interest in divination? For we can change nothing. But foreknowledge has some utility, for we may be more prepared or not prepared to co-operate with the future events.

[38] Not only divination, but also prayers and the rituals of priests can have an effect on the future. Many people could escape from an evil threatening them in the future thanks to prophecy.

[39] Proclus examines in what cases divination and sacred rituals can be effective regarding future events, in what cases they cannot.

3. Problem: one vital force penetrating the universe

[40] One vital force coming from the celestial ether penetrates the universe. All living beings receive life from it according to their corporeal capacities. The same vital force is, in the brain, rational life, in the senses, sensitive.

[41] *Ad hominem* argument against Theodore: how can a great mathematician depreciate the intellectual life and class it together with sense perception? There is a great opposition between sensible and intellectual life.

[42] It is absurd to let the essence of the soul emanate from ether. Even if you consider the ether itself as ensouled, the source of the souls is established before the ether and ethereal souls. Explanation of the 'mixing bowl' of *Timaeus*.

[43] Other *ad hominem* argument: the mathematical sciences should have taught Theodore how to transcend the sensible divisible objects.

[44] The sensible life is ruled by fate for it is inseparable from matter and extrinsically moved. The rational life does not depend on sense perception and its violent affects. It transcends body and is self-activating. To this life we must attribute choice, which may tend upwards and downwards, according to the intermediary status of the soul.

4. Intermezzo: hedonism

[45] Problem: 'the good is what is pleasurable to each individual and is so by convention: for different customs prevail among different people'. Proclus is ashamed to discuss at his age this hedonistic relativism. The good is by nature the same for all humans and cannot be identified with the pleasures the masses pursue.

[46] This absurd view is connected with the preceding. For if the rational soul is ranked together with the irrational perceptions, the good and the pleasurable seem to be identical. But we must not be emulators of the cattle but of the gods. No need to repeat the numerous arguments of Plato against the identification of the good with the pleasurable.

[47] One should explain the manifold differences in human customs as the result of different types of lives according to the dominance of a kind of soul: the rational, the irascible, and the appetitive. What is pleasurable is diverse for different people, but what is good is only given to those people in whom reason dominates the passions.

5. Problem: scepticism

[48] Problem: (1) Socrates says that he knows nothing, (2) maintains that we shall only know the truth when we depart from here, (3) and even affirms that the mathematical sciences are not really sciences. Theodore concludes that it is impossible to know the truth in this life.
Reply: This is not an argument against free choice. If we cannot know the truth, it is also impossible to know whether we are free or not free in our choices.

[49] (against arg. 2.) We have to distinguish different forms of knowledge, some can be obtained in this life, some only after this life.

[50] (against arg. 3) Socrates refuses to call the mathematical sciences 'sciences' because they fall short of the supreme science (dialectic).

[51] (against arg. 1) Explanation of Socratic ignorance. The fact of not knowing is not as such a special privilege, but rather, when not knowing, to know that one does not know. This ignorance presupposes knowledge of oneself.

[52] Plato is not a sceptical philosopher: 'For it is Plato himself who claims that anyone who abolishes science could not assert anything about whatsoever.'

6. Problem: misfortune of good people

[53] Problem: 'why do the good fare badly, failing to achieve the goals they have set, whereas the bad achieve what they desire?'
This is not an argument against free choice. The ancient philosophers have put it forward, not in order to destroy that which depends on us, but rather to examine providence.

[54] This is not a valid argument against free choice; on the contrary, it

Introduction

can be made an argument for its existence. For if we had no free choice, if we were not morally responsible, it would no longer make sense to protest about the outcome of events, saying that they occur contrary to merit.

[55] The faculty that depends on us is not a power ruling over external events, but only collaborating with them. It has absolute power only over that which is internal to the soul. Epictetus teaches us to distinguish between what depends on us and what does not depend on us.

7. Problem: the power of self-determination is a divine privilege

[56] Having defined that which depends on us as 'that which is by nothing dominated or mastered, but is self-determined and self-activated' Theodore concludes that only the divinity can possess such an absolute power of self-determination.

[57] Proclus objects that this definition goes against the traditional understanding of it. Philosophers always understood 'what depends on us' as referring to the activity of choice. They did not identify choice (*proairesis*) and will (*boulêsis*): the will, they say, only regards the good, whereas choice is likewise of good and not good things. The ambivalent inclination of choice is characteristic of the soul, which holds an intermediary place between the intelligible and the sensible.

[58] A definition of choice. Choice is a rational appetitive faculty that strives for some good, either true or apparent.

[59] Because of the ambivalent inclination of this faculty the soul may ascend or descend. This faculty is characteristic of human souls: it belongs neither to gods nor to mortal beings.

[60] We humans are intermediate beings established in the faculty of choice. Therefore, what depends on us cannot be understood as the power and licence to do whatever we want. Only the gods have such a power. We may share it when we live a godlike life.

[61] Theodore erroneously attributes to the human soul a power to lead all things in accordance with its impulses. However, what is outside does not depend on us. Our life is a mixture of what depends on us and what does not depend on us. Virtuous people acquire the greatest freedom.

8. Problem: divine providence excludes human freedom

[62] If God knows whatever will happen, we have to admit that all things are necessitated.

[63] Opposing views of the Peripatetics and the Stoics. In order to preserve contingency the former declare that god knows future events only in an indeterminate way. The latter attribute to god determinate knowledge of the future, but thus reduce all things to necessity. But the Platonists reconcile future contingency with determinate divine foreknowledge.

[64] The form of knowledge must not correspond to what the object of knowledge is, but to what the subject of knowledge is.

[65] Therefore, it is not true that, if the gods know the future, its outcome is by necessity fixed, but one should attribute to the future an indeterminate outcome from what is determinate, and to the gods a determinate foreknowledge of what is indeterminate. Example of the astronomical clock.

Conclusion: the gods know what depends on us in a divine and timeless manner and yet we act according to our nature. And whatever we choose is foreknown by them, not because of a determination in us, but of one in them.

Conclusion

[66] Thus far Proclus' answers to Theodore's questions. He could have developed many more arguments for free choice, demonstrating the unfortunate practical consequences of a deterministic worldview. Proclus encourages Theodore to study those arguments, but also asks him to take distance from the sophistic reasoning coming from the deterministic philosophers.

Notes

1. See Westerink (1962), 162-3, and Saffrey (1992).
2. See Marinus, *Vita Procli* §15,15-17 with n. 2 (on pp. 119-20).
3. According to Marinus, the commentary on the *Timaeus* was one of the first works of Proclus (*Vita Procli* §13). It seems probable, however, that Proclus reworked it later (see the note at §13,14-17, on p. 112). In his commentary on the *Republic*, Proclus refers to it as an already published work (*in Remp.* II 335,20: *ekdidomenois*).
4. There are also parallels between the discussion on evil in *De Mal.* and in this commentary, see, for instance, *in Remp.* I 37,23-39,1 and Festugière (1970), vol. 1, p. 54, n. 4 and p. 55, n. 1.
5. On the history of the transmission of the *Tria Opuscula*, see the introduction of the English translation of *De Mal.*, Opsomer-Steel (2003), 1-9.
6. See Isaac (1979).
7. See Boese (1960), Erler (1979) and (1980). The translation of Erler has extensive notes, which were often useful in the preparation of my annotations.
8. Unfortunately, this is also the defect of the new Italian translation of the *opuscula* by Paparella (2004).

Introduction

9. For the year of Syrianus' death, see Saffrey-Westerink (1968), xvi-xvii; Cardullo (1995), 22-4.

10. On eclecticism as a philosophical position, see Dillon-Long (1988).

11. *De Prov.* 1,12-19.

12. See Long-Sedley (1987), §55.

13. See Sharples (1983), 9 with n. 42.

14. On the Stoic attempts to reconcile determinism and freedom, see Bobzien (1998), Hankinson (1999), and, more recently, Salles (2005).

15. On the discussion of fate and providence by Platonists, see Dörrie-Baltes (1993), 86-8; 320-7; Schibli (2002), 129-63; Dragona-Monachou (1994), 4417-90; Sorabji (2004b), 79-133.

16. On Alcinous' doctrine on fate and providence, see Mansfeld (1999).

17. See Proclus, *in Remp.* II 357,28ff.; for more references see Sorabji, (2004b), 131-3. For Calcidius see den Boeft (1970).

18. Nemesius, *De Nat. Hom.* 38, p. 109,17-18; see also [Plut.], *De Fato* 573B.

19. Calcidius, *in Tim.* 143, p. 182,4-5; 146, p. 185,2.

20. In my presentation of this work, I follow Sharples' (1983) introduction to his edition.

21. Sharples (1983), 19-21.

22. Alexander's treatise *On Providence* only survives in an Arabic translation: see Thillet (2003). Alexander seems to defend the Aristotelian doctrine against the unfair cricism of the Platonists in the second century: see Atticus, fr. 3 des Places.

23. Lewy (1978), 365ff. On Hecate, see Johnston (1990). Proclus' theological interpretation of Hecate is discussed by Van den Berg (2001), 252ff.

24. Plotinus III 1 [3] 8,1-3.

25. See also the treatise *On Astrology* (Plotinus II 3 [52]) and the arguments in the first treatise of the *Questions on the Soul* (Plotinus IV 3 [27] 8-9). On Plotinus' doctrine on Fate and Providence, see Russi (2004).

26. The treatise is preserved by Stobaeus, *Anth.* II 8,39-42 (= fr. 268-71, Smith). For a French translation, see Festugière (1970), vol. 3, pp. 349-57. Cf. Dörrie-Baltes (2002b), 'Baustein' 174, 3-4 with commentary on pp. 264-71.

27. On the *Sentences* of Porphyry, see Brisson *et al.* (2005) and especially the contribution of C. D'Ancona in that volume.

28. *Letter to Macedonius* (= Stobaeus, *Anth.* II 173,3-176,21 W.-H.); *Letter to Sopater* (= Stobaeus, *Anth.* I 81,7-18 W.-H.). J. Dillon has published a translation of the fragments from the letter to Macedonius in Dillon-Gerson (2004), 244-8.

29. Stobaeus, *Anth.* II 173,29 W.-H., trans. J. Dillon.

30. Stobaeus, *Anth.* II 173,5-17 W.-H., trans. J. Dillon.

31. On Hierocles and his treatise on Providence, see now Schibli (2002).

32. Aulus Gellius, *Noct. Attic.* 7.2.1. See also Alexander, *De Anima mantissa* 185,1ff. (= *SVF* 2.920).

33. Alexander, *De Fato* 22, p. 191,30-192,8; trans. Sharples (1983), 70 with commentary on pp. 152-4.

34. On the etymological connection between *heirmos* and *heimarmenê* see Alexander, *Aporiae* 9,26 (= *SVF* 2.962); Nemesius, *De Nat. Hom.* 37, p. 108,16 (= *SVF* 2.918); Gregory of Nyssa, *Contra Fatum* 35,14; Plotinus III 1 [3] 4,10-11; and Proclus, *in Remp.* II 29,10-11 and *in Tim.* III 272,24.

35. For the characterisation of fate as *aparabatos* and *anapodrastos* in a Stoic context, see *SVF* 2.528, 917, 918, 960, 1000; see also Nemesius, *De Nat. Hom.* 36, p. 108,17; 37, p. 109,12-13; Marcus Aurelius 12.1. See also Sharples (1983),

126 with further references. The term *anapodrastos* is connected with the mythological figure of Adrasteia in Ps.-Aristotle, *De Mundo* 401b13.

36. Plotinus III 1 [3] 2,30-5.
37. *De Prov.* 3,3-5.
38. Epictetus, *Ench.* 17 and Marcus Aurelius 11.6, 12.36.
39. Alexander, *De Fato* 31, p. 202,21-2.
40. Our passage is probably influenced by Plotinus III 2 [47] 15,21 and 17,16-34, as already noted by Boese. Plotinus himself adopted the simile from Stoicism. On the importance of this metaphor, see Reis (2000).
41. cf. Plotinus III 8 [30] 2,3 and Proclus, *in Tim.* I 297,28; 395,28; *in Parm.* IV 878,4.
42. *De Prov.* 65,4-5.
43. See Bobzien (1998) and Salles (2005).
44. Thus Alexander, *De Fato* 14, p. 182,22-4.
45. Plotinus III 1 [3] 7,15. The same statement can be found in Simplicius, *in Epict.* 1,445 (p. 25, ed. I. Hadot).
46. Firmicus Maternus, *Mathesis*, I 7,14-22 (on Plotinus) and I 8,3: 'omnia vero quae ad cursum uitae pertinent in nostra volunt esse posita potestate, ut nostrum sit quod uiuimus, fati uero ac sortis solum uideatur esse quod morimur'.
47. Christian authors in late Antiquity continued in many ways the philosophical debate on determinism and human freedom. They thoughtfully exploited arguments from the Academy, from Platonists and Aristotelians in order to defend moral responsibility against determinists (in most cases astrological determinists). For a survey of this discussion, see Amand (1945).
48. On Gregory's treatise see Amand (1945), 423-39.
49. *De Prov.* 3,1-4,3.
50. See *De Prov.* 15 and n. 65 of the translation.
51. Proclus distinguishes the same levels in *in Alc.* 245,6-248,4 (cf. the annotations of Segonds, who indicates several parallels).
52. Plato, *Resp.* 10, 619C (trans. P. Shorey).
53. Plato, *Leg.* 5, 727B (trans. T. Saunders).
54. Epictetus, *Ench.* 5 (trans. W. Oldfather).
55. *in Alc.* 287,2-8 (trans. W. O'Neill). See Segond's important 'note complémentaire' 1 (p. 440), where parallel texts are quoted. See also Simplicius, *in Epict.* 11 (p. 65ff., ed. I. Hadot and p. 158, n. 1).
56. Plato, *Alc.* 113C4. Cf. Proclus, *in Alc.* 292,17-26 with reference to *Resp.* 10, 619C5-6.
57. See Eusebius, *Praep. Evang.* 4.3.1 (= *SVF* 2.939; Long-Sedley (1987), §55 P); cf. also Cicero, *De Divinatione* 1.127 (= *SVF* 2.944; Long-Sedley (1987), §55 O).
58. See Cicero, *De Divinatione* 1.125-6 and Pease's commentary ad loc. (pp. 320-1).
59. Alexander, *De Fato* 31, p. 202,1ff., trans. Sharples (1983), and his commentary on pp. 166-8.
60. See Calcidius, *in Tim.* 161, p. 194,20-2.
61. Diogenes Laertius 7.139 (see also Long-Sedley (1987), §48 O and Clemens Alex., *Stromata* 5.8, p. 674). On the Neoplatonic interpretation of the containing cause, see Steel (2003).
62. See Iamblichus, *De Anima* 9, p. 32,11 (ed. Finamore and Dillon) and their commentary on pp. 95-100.
63. See Plotinus III 1 [3] 4,1ff. (and n. 1 in Armstrong's translation).
64. Cf. Tieleman (1996), 38ff.

65. See also Proclus, *in Alc.* 260,2-6; 327,24-5.

66. On this argument of Carneades and its influence in the later anti-deterministic debate, in particular among Christians, see Amand (1945), 55-60.

67. See Anonymous, *in Theaet.* 54-5, pp. 143-4, and Sedley (1996).

68. cf. Cicero, *Acad.* 1.12.44-5.

69. On this question, see Opsomer (1998) and Bonazzi (2003).

70. Proclus, *in Eucl.* 29,14-32,20.

71. Proclus, *De Prov.* 48,6-11.

72. Sextus Empiricus, *Pyrr. Hyp.* 1.32.

73. See also Plotinus III 2 [47] 6,1ff.

74. In his edition of Damascius, Combès translates 'ce qui se circonscrit soi-même'. Cf. *in Parm.*, II, p. 100, n. 2; III, p. 23, n. 4.

75. In *De Prov.* 10,19 and 12,22, he calls 'fate' the 'ruler' of the corporeal realm.

76. Plotinus VI 8 [39] 1,16-20, trans. Armstrong, modified.

77. See Simplicius, *in Epict.* 1,133-221 (pp. 12-16, ed. I. Hadot).

78. On this debate in Late Antiquity, and in particular on the confrontation of Alexander and Proclus, see Mignucci (1985) and Sorabji (1983), ch. 16, and (2004b), 69-78. On Boethius' views and on his antecedents, see Gruber's (1978) commentary on the fifth book; see also Marenbon (2003).

79. Alexander, *De Fato* 30, p. 200,28ff., trans. Sharples (1983); see also his commentary on p. 164ff. as well as his introduction on p. 28 with n. 197. See, moreover, *SVF* 2.963. Because the Stoics identified providence with necessity, they absolished all forms of contingency. See, finally, the long discussion in Cicero's *De Divinatione* 2.15 with the commentary of Pease ad loc. (p. 372ff.).

80. *De Prov.* 6,2-7, cf. Sorabji (2004b), 76.

81. Alexander, *De Fato* 30, p. 201,15-18, trans. Sharples (1983); see also his commentary on p. 165 with references to the later debate in the Neoplatonic school.

82. *Elem. Theol.* §124 (trans. Dodds; see also his commentary on p. 266, where he points out that Proclus is answering here to the objection raised in Plato, *Parm.* 134Cff.).

83. *De Prov.* 7,34-5. On the contrast between Proclus and Porphyry, see Proclus, *in Tim.* I 352,5-16. The latter text is also quoted by Sorabji (2004b), 73.

84. Alexander, *De Fato* 16-21, pp. 186,13-191,25.

85. Seneca, *Ep. Mor.* 16.4.

86. The last section of the Latin text is difficult to interpret. In particular, the reference to the Stoics depends on a conjecture. For a justification of this conjecture, see the Philological Appendix.

PROCLUS
On Providence

Translation

PROCLUS
On providence and fate and what depends on us
A reply to Theodore the engineer

Introduction

1. The labours[1] of your soul, my friend Theodore, seem to have brought about insights that are mature and fitting for a man who loves to investigate reality. I appreciate that you thought you should write also to us about these matters, though there are many competent people around you who could investigate and examine such problems together with you. But we too, so it seems, should expound our views concerning the questions you sent us and say what we consider to be in accordance with reality and with the most illustrious of former philosophers. We should listen to your queries carefully, since they come from a man who is expert in the mechanical sciences and who is, I believe, an old friend, as you yourself mention in your letter.

The questions you ask are about problems that have been discussed a thousand times and will, in my opinion, never cease to challenge the soul to investigate them. They have indeed already been examined by many:[2] they have been discussed by the famous Plotinus and Iamblichus, and before them in the writings of the divine Plato, as also, if I may express my opinion, before Plato in the revelations made by theologians who proclaimed 'with a delirious mouth'[3] what Plato has established by more sober demonstrations. And what need is there to bring forward Plato and the experts in divine matters? The gods themselves, who know their own affairs clearly[4] and also which and what kind of things they produced after themselves, have openly expressed their views, and not in riddles, as do the theologians.[5]

2. Following them, we too, as I have said, must explain to you in writing the matters about which you have questions. The [error] you suffer from is worthy of forgiveness. Considering the *mise en scène* of human affairs in all sorts of ways, tragic and comic,[6] you believed that the one maker and producer of all those scenes resides solely in the universe, and you called this cause 'fate' (*heimarmenê*); or rather, taking 'fate' to be the connection (*heirmos*) itself of those scenes and the ordered sequence of events, you supposed that this dramaturgy is directed merely by some kind of unalterable necessity;[7] and the latter you celebrate as providence, considering it the only self-determining power (*autexousion*) and mistress of all things, whereas the self-determination of the human soul, about which there is so much talk, is in your opinion only a name and nothing in reality. For the soul is situated in the world and subservient to the actions of other things and is a part of the functioning of the cosmos. Rather, to use your own words, the inescapable cause, which moves all things that this cosmos 'comprehends within itself',[8] is 'mechanic', and the universe is, as it were, one machine, wherein the celestial spheres are analogous to the interlocking wheels and the particular beings, the animals and the souls, are like the things moved by the wheels, and everything depends upon one moving principle.[9] Perhaps you have entertained such views to honour your own discipline, considering the maker of the universe to be some kind of engineer and yourself as the imitator of 'the best of all causes'.[10]

3. But this we wrote, as it were, mixing play with serious matters.[11] Let us now enter the discussion. It is my view that, if you want to track down[12] the problems under investigation, you should above all examine the following three distinctions.[13]

First is the distinction between providence and fate. They are not distinguished as you formulate it in your letter, making the latter *the connected sequence*, the former the *necessity causing this* [sequence]. Rather, they are both causes of the world and of the things that take place in the world. However, providence precedes fate, and everything that comes about according to fate, comes about far more according to providence. The converse, however, is not true, for the supreme divisions of the universe are ruled by providence, which is more divine than fate.

The *second* distinction is that between two types of soul. The one is separable from the body and descends into 'this mortal region'[14] from somewhere above, from the gods; the other is that which resides in the bodies and is inseparable from its substrates. The latter depends in its being upon fate, the former upon providence.

The *third* distinction concerns knowledge and truth. One type [of knowledge] exists in souls that are engaged in the process of generation, though they may live an immaculate life, another type is present in souls that have escaped from this place and are established 'there' from where for them began the fall, the 'moulting of the feathers',[15] and the descent into 'this mortal region'.

4. If you sufficiently grasp the three distinctions we mentioned, the solution to all the problems you raised will become clear. For given that providence differs from fate, as stated above, it will be evident how many things escape fate, but nothing providence, and furthermore how providence governs from above over fate, which it itself produced, and how it entrusts to it [fate] the authority as far as the bodies that are externally moved (or those things that first come to be in externally moved things).[16] Once it is demonstrated that there are two souls, one separable from bodies and another 'implanted in bodies',[17] it will become

clear to you which of them has self-determination and that which depends on us, and which is subservient to necessity and is drawn under fate; and where these souls are interwoven so that the one dims self-determination because of the inferior life, whereas the other participates in some likeness of choice because it is adjacent to the superior soul. Finally, when you will have seen that knowledge is twofold, it will be evident what both Plato and Socrates say – and the great Parmenides should be added to them[18] – namely that the soul, even when dwelling here, knows the truth, when it is purified from the material darkness and the affections that the body and its mixture with the body wipe off upon it;[19] and that it has a better and purer share in what is 'really true knowledge',[20] once being outside of bodies and generation and 'bitter matter'.[21]

5a. These three problems, then, are necessary [preambles for the following discussion] and have been fully discussed by the ancient philosophers.[22] The first has been elaborated by Iamblichus in his innumerable arguments on providence and fate. The second has been examined by all Platonists who claim that there is a twofold soul. The third has often been discussed by Plotinus, often also by Porphyry: they both distinguish between the act of contemplation and the contemplative virtue.[23] But Plato has treated all three problems, if one is capable of following him.

Part I. Three preliminary distinctions

1. The distinction between providence and fate

5b. It is necessary, then, to begin with the first problem and to find the difference between providence and fate. As Plato says, 'in every case', my friend, 'there is one starting point, to know what the theory is about; otherwise one risks complete failure'.[24] One must also, as the ingenious Aristotle[25] teaches, after investigating *whether* something exists examine next *what* it is.[26] Therefore, if you were investigating whether providence exists or not, and similarly about fate, it would first have to be demonstrated to you that both exist, and if you were still in doubt about them, I had wished to uphold the argument to you that they do exist. But since you too agree that they both exist and contend that all things are necessary because of their domination, the next step, I believe, is evident: I have to explain *what* each of them is, and from this it will also become clear how they differ from one another. Once this is known, many of your problems will be solved, as we have said.

6. Furthermore, since the method of division is said to contribute to the discovery of what a thing is – hence, Socrates in the *Philebus* exalted this method as 'a gift from the gods to humans'[27] – and since also our so-called common notions,[28] starting from which we can track[29] many of the theorems to be demonstrated, as Aristotle wrote,[30] contribute to the definition of the principles, we too have to use both procedures in order to establish what we call providence and fate. On the one hand, we shall use the common notions we have about them, on the other hand, the divisions of beings 'according to articulations'.[31] Only when starting from them, it seems to me, will we discover what the definition is of fate and providence. Once known, they will kindle a bright light[32] upon the matters under investigation: and maybe they will be sufficient for us who right now tackle the problems about them.

7. These, then, are said to be the common notions about fate and providence present in all souls without having been taught: providence is the cause of goods for those governed by it; fate also is a cause, but of some connection between and sequence of things that occur. That we all have these uncorrupted notions about fate and providence, we show in the way we speak. For we say of people who have constituted themselves as 'providers' (*proxenoi*) of the good for others whatever that may be[33] that they exercise providence for those who have benefited from them. Again, when something happens through many causes that are interconnected and unknown to us, we invariably call this fate (*heimarmenê*).[34] Our lives are filled with such words, since the words too bear witness to these [innate] notions. For the term *pro-noia* (pro-vidence or thinking in advance) plainly signifies the activity before the intellect,[35] which must be attributed solely to the Good – for only the Good is more divine than the intellect, since even the much praised intellect desires the Good together with all things and before all things.[36] The term *heimarmenê* (fate) indicates the cause that strings together all things that are destined to have such a connection. This is also evident from the names the experts in divine matters use. For they speak of some allotted *klôstêres* (threads of fate) and *nêmata* (yarns) of the Moirai,[37] by which – in my opinion – they also mean the sequence (*heirmos*) of all concatenated events, which fate imposes upon them as the one transcendent cause of the connected things.

8. Besides, providence is not identical with what is subject to providence nor yet is it the gift coming down to it, but it is the 'providing' cause; and fate is not what is connected, nor the connection coming into it, but the connecting principle. You may come to understand this from the fact that we all imagine providence and fate to be an efficient agency. But it is a general law that efficient causes are distinct from their effects. The following three, then, differ from one another: the efficient cause, the effect, the efficient activity. In this case too, are to be distinguished: the 'providing' cause, that which is subject to providence, and the activity that goes from the providing cause to its subject; and also: the connecting principle, that which is connected, and the activity proceeding from

the connecting principle to that which is connected. It is also evident that in each of those triads the efficient cause does not have the same properties as its effect.[38] If the effect is complex, its efficient cause must be simple, if the effect shares in some good, the efficient cause must be this good unparticipated. For in all cases the efficient cause has been allotted a more 'divine role'[39] than its effect. Hence by calling providence the cause of good things, we shall declare that it is the source of good things and thus does not need other things to make it good; and by positing fate as the cause of connection, we shall not say that it is itself connected by other things.

Such, then, are the common notions that we have *a priori* of fate and providence. Let us next investigate over which domain each of them rules, and first the domain of fate. Starting from those innate notions we have established that fate is the cause of connected events. But let us now turn to the question as to what those connected things are.

9. Of all beings, some have their substance in eternity, others in time.[40] In eternity are those beings that have an activity coeternal with their substance, in time, those whose substance 'is not but always comes to be', even if it exits for an infinite time.[41] Other beings are somehow intermediary between them: they have a substance that is stable and better than becoming, but an activity that is always becoming; their substance is measured by eternity, their activity by time. For every procession must proceed from the first to the lowest degrees through intermediaries.[42] As there are beings that are eternal in both respects [sc. in substance and in activities] and beings that need time in both respects, there must also be some intermediary realm, which either has an eternal substance and a temporal activity or the other way around. But the latter alternative is not possible, for otherwise we run the risk of putting activities before substances. The only remaining possibility is to make the intermediary eternal in substance, temporal in activity. Thus, we have pointed out to you the three orders of beings, which we call intellectual, psychic, and corporeal. By the 'intellectual' I mean the order that both exists and thinks in eternity; by 'corporeal', the order that is always becoming either for infinite time or for a part of time; by 'psychic', the order that is eternal in substance, but uses temporal activities.

10. Where, then, should you put the things that are interconnected by fate (*eiromena*)? Examine the question, taking from the terms the meaning of what is to be connected (*eiresthai*). The term *eiresthai* indicates nothing other than that different things happening at different times are linked with one another and not isolated; and that, when they occur at the same time, though dissociated in place, they are somehow co-ordinated with one another. Hence, whether they are separated in place or in time, they are somehow brought into unity and into a single sympathy[43] through the *heirmos* or connection. In general, connected things cannot have this state on their own account, but they need another cause that provides them with this *heirmos* or connection. According, then, to our common notion of 'fate', events that are ordered under fate are those that are interconnected; and according to the generally accepted understanding of 'connection', interconnected things are divided, dissociated either in place or time, though capable of being connected by another cause. Such things are moved by another and are corporeal. For things existing outside of bodies are either superior to both place and time or, if they have activities in time, seem at least not to occupy space.[44] From all these premises the conclusion is evident: things governed and connected by fate must be things moved by an external cause and totally corporeal. And if this is established, it is clear that, in laying down fate as the cause of the connection, we shall posit it as the 'patron'[45] of things that are externally moved and corporeal.

11. Taking this standpoint, we shall now ask ourselves what is said to be and really is the proximate cause of bodies and by what cause externally moved bodies are moved, animated and maintained,[46] insofar as is possible for them. Let us look first, if you agree, at our own bodies and see what the cause is that moves them and nourishes them and 'weaves them anew'[47] and preserves them. Is this not also the vegetative power, which serves a similar purpose in the other living beings, including those rooted in earth [i.e. the plants]?[48] It has a twofold activity: one is to renew that which is extinguished in the bodies, in order that they may not be dispersed entirely; the other to maintain each body in its natural condition. For to add what is lacking is not the same as to preserve the power of the bodies maintained by it. If, then, not only in us and in the other animals and plants, but also in this whole world there exists, prior to bodies, the single nature of the world, which maintains the constitution of the bodies and moves them, as is also the case in human beings – for how else could we call all bodies 'offspring' of nature?[49] –, this nature must be the cause of connected things and in this we must search for what we call fate. Maybe it is for this reason that the ingenious Aristotle used to call increases and generations that occur at abnormal times, 'contrary to fate' (*par' heimarmenên*).[50] The divine Plato also says that the whole world, when it is considered in itself as a corporeal entity without the intellectual gods, 'lets fate and its own inborn urge retake control'.[51] In agreement with these thinkers the gods declare in the Oracles: 'do not gaze at nature: its name is fate',[52] thereby confirming our demonstrations.

12. Thus we have discovered the meaning of fate and how it is the nature of this world,[53] an incorporeal substance, as the patron of bodies, and life as well as substance, since it moves bodies from the inside and not from the outside, moving everything according to time and connect-

ing the movements of all things that are dissociated in time and place. According to fate mortal beings are also connected with eternal beings and are set in rotation together with them,[54] and all are in mutual sympathy.[55] Also nature in us binds together all the parts of our body and connects their interaction, and this nature can also be viewed as a kind of 'fate' of our body. For just as in our body some parts are more important and others less important and the latter follow the former, so too in the entire universe: the generations of the less important parts follow the movements of the more important, for instance, the generations of the sublunary bodies follow the rotations of the celestial bodies. And circularity down here is an image of the circle there in the eternal realm. However, since all this has often been discussed by the ancients,[56] I do not wish to develop the theme further.

13. It is not difficult for you to understand what providence is, which we call the 'source of goods'.[57] If you define it first as a divine cause, you will be right. For from where else than from god can come what is good for all things? Hence, as Plato says, 'for good things, we must invoke no other cause than god'.[58] Next you have to admit that, since it presides over both the intelligible and the sensible realm, it is superior to fate. For events that fall under fate also fall under providence: they have their interconnection from fate, but their orientation to the good comes from providence. Thus, the connection will have the good as its end and providence will order fate. On the other hand, things that fall under providence do not all need fate as well; for intelligible beings transcend fate. Where indeed could fate be in the incorporeal things, if it introduces together with connection both time and corporeal movement? It was in view of this situation, I believe, that Plato too said that 'the constitution of this world is a mixture of intellect and necessity, whereby intellect rules over necessity'.[59] Plato calls 'necessity' the moving cause of the bodies, which he calls 'fate' in other texts,[60] and he allows bodies that are moved by it to be necessitated by it. And rightly so, for every body is necessitated to do what it does and to undergo what it undergoes, to heat or to be heated, to cool or to be cooled.[61] There is no choice in bodies.[62] Hence you might say that necessity and the absence of choice is a characteristic of bodies, but not something better than bodies. For even what moves in a circle, moves of necessity in this way, since it has a nature capable of a circular movement, just as fire moves to the circumference and earth to the centre.[63] Thus Plato set necessity to preside over the coming to be of bodies, and hence also over their passing away. But he removed intellect from it, ordering it to rule over necessity. If, then, providence is superior even to intellect, it is evident that it rules over intellect and over all those things subject to necessity, and that necessity rules only over the things subject to it. Thus, everything that is of an intellectual nature falls only under providence, whereas everything that exists in a corporeal way, falls also under necessity.

14. You should therefore consider that there are two realms, the intelligible and the sensible, each with its own kingdom, that of providence above ruling over the intelligible and the sensible, that of fate below ruling over the sensible. Providence is to be distinguished from fate, as god differs from what is divine, [i.e.] divine by participation and not primarily. For in other cases also, as you can see, there is a difference between that which is primary and that which is by participation, for example the light which the sun is and the light in the air, the former being primarily light and the latter light because of the former. Life also is primarily in the soul, and secondarily in the body because of the soul. Thus, providence is *per se* god, whereas fate is something divine, but not god. This is because it depends upon providence and is as it were an image of it. For if providence is to intelligible beings as fate is to sensible beings – the former reigns over the intellectual realm, the latter over the sensible –, then, inversely, as the geometers say,[64] as providence is to fate, so too are intelligible objects to sensible objects. But the intelligible beings are beings in the primary sense and the sensible derive from them. Hence, providence is what it is primarily, and the order of fate depends upon it.

2. The distinction between separable and inseparable souls

15. But enough about this topic. Let us now proceed, if you agree, to our second investigation, namely that concerning [the two kinds of soul], one that is separable from bodies and another that is inseparable. Take then this principle also from the philosophy of Aristotle![65] He says that every soul with an activity that does not need body is also endowed with a substance of this kind, free from body and separable. This is necessarily the case. For if we bring the substance of the soul down to the level of the body, whereas its activity occurs without a body, then the activity will be superior to the substance, since it will need nothing of the inferior to be in its natural state, whereas the substance will be rooted in it. But this is impossible. Therefore, the soul that can act separately from the body must also have an existence separable from the body.

16. Examine then, my friend, which of the souls in us we shall admit does not need body to exercise its natural activities. Could it be sense perception? Clearly not, as every sensitive faculty uses bodies as organs and is active with them regarding its proper sense objects, undergoing change and being affected together with the eyes and ears and all the other sense organs. Well then, could it be anger and desire? But, you see that these too often work together with such bodily parts as the heart and the liver,[66] and that they are not free from bodies. And how could faculties that are active together with sense perception not need a body, since perception is always moved through a body? That the appetitive faculties operate with perception, we all, I believe, know. For how could

one get angry about what is not perceived? And what could one desire? As Plotinus rightly says, 'affections are either perceptions or not without perceptions'.[67] Hence, if both the irascible and the appetitive part are accompanied by perception – the irascible has the perception of what is painful, the appetitive part of what is pleasurable – and if what acts with perception acts with body – for perception goes together with body – then every irascible and appetitive faculty must act together with body. Accordingly, these forms of life, which are all irrational, have their natural activity together with body.

17. And now look up at the rational soul itself and consider its life, the third [from below] but also the first,[68] riding upon the inferior lives;[69] it either corrects what is deficient in their knowledge, as when it refutes from above perception that is deceived in regard to its own objects, as for instance, when perception declares that the sun is only a foot in diameter,[70] or expresses a similar illusion coming from the sensible objects with the usual deceit; or it educates the immoderate character of emotions, when it strikes the irascible part, shouting the Homeric words 'endure, my heart'[71] and drawing it back from its impulses, as if it were a raging dog; or again when it attempts to contain the desire that springs up[72] on the occasion of the pleasures that burst forth from bodies, warding off their spell[73] with temperance. In all such activities, the rational soul shows that it disdains all irrational motions, both cognitive and appetitive, and liberates itself from them as though they were alien. Now, when searching for the nature of something, one should start not from those activities that make a perverted use of it, but from those that act according to nature. When, then, reason in us functions as reason, it rebukes the illusory painting of the pleasures of desire,[74] chastises the impetuous movement of the irascible part, disdains perception as full of illusions, saying that 'we neither hear nor see anything accurate',[75] and declares this, looking at its internal reasons, none of which could be seen through the body or bodily cognitions.[76] Hence, it is clear that the soul acting in that way manifestly dissociates itself from sense perceptions, which it condemns, and from the pleasure and pain, which it eliminates.

18. Consider after this another and better activity of the rational soul in us, where the inferior faculties are already at rest and make no noise, such as that usually found among the masses.[77] It is the movement by which the soul reflects upon itself and sees its own essence, the powers in itself, the harmonic proportions of which it consists[78] and the many lives of which it is the plenitude; and it discovers that it is itself a rational world,[79] the image of the beings before it, of which it 'leapt out',[80] and the paradigm of things after it, which it presides over. Arithmetic, my friend, and geometry, the mother of your discipline,[81] are both said to contribute much to this activity of the soul. They detach it from sense perceptions, purify the intellect from confused irrational forms of life, lead it on to grasp the incorporeal forms, as, before the most sacred rituals, lustral water is offered to those who are to be initiated.[82] Consider indeed how these sciences, which are established prior to [purely] intellectual activities, have come to possess the purifying power we mentioned.[83] For when they receive the soul filled with images, which does not know anything clearly and without the confusion caused by matter, they display arguments that have the irrefutable necessity of demonstrations and forms filled with all precision and immateriality, which in no way draw over them the vagueness found in sensible objects. How, then, would they not purify our intellectual life from the things that fill us with stupidity and at the same time lead it to the vantage-point[84] of divine beings?

19. After both of these activities, as stated, of this rational soul, let us ascend to its supreme intellection, by which it views its sister souls in the world,[85] who have been allotted the heavens and the entire world of becoming, according to the will of the Father. As it is in a way a part of them itself, it desires to share their view. And it sees above the souls all the orders of the intellectual beings. For above every soul a godlike intellect is superposed, which grants it an intellectual disposition. Next, it sees prior to them the monads of the gods themselves above the intellect, from which the intellectual multitudes receive their unification. For above all unified things there must be established unifying causes, just as above beings made alive, the causes of life, and above beings made intellectual, the causes of intellect and, in general, above all participating beings, the unparticipated hypostases. Following all of these anagogic insights, I make it clear, I think, for all those who are not completely blind, that the soul, having abandoned sense perception below as well as the bodies, breaks forth from the vantage-point[86] of its intellectual part into a Bacchic frenzy[87] at the calm and truly mystical intuitions of the hypercosmic gods. For from where, from what sort of activities have the 'offspring of the gods'[88] revealed to us the invisible orders of the gods? How are souls said to be possessed by the gods and in contact with them, having taken on 'madness'?[89] I mean, for example, the Sibyl, who, as it is told, began to say wondrous things soon after her birth and those present could hear from her who she was and from what [divine] order she came into this place on earth?[90] Or some other soul, if there has been one that partakes in so much divine nature.[91]

20. To summarise: whenever the rational and intellectual soul moves somehow according to its nature, it gets outside of bodies and beyond sense perceptions. Hence, it must also have a substance that is separable from both. After this has become clear, it will by now be evident of itself that, when the soul acts according to its nature, it is superior to the condition of being led by fate; but when it is brought down to sense perception and made irrational and corporeal, it goes along with the things below, lives together with them as with some drunken neighbours,[92] and it is dominated by the cause that reigns over them. For there must exist also such a class of beings that are in their substance above fate, but are sometimes placed under fate through relation.[93] For if there are some beings that are for all eternity established above 'the laws of fate',[94] and others that are for all their life subordinated to the periods of fate, then, there must indeed be a nature intermediary between them, a nature that is sometimes outside the action of fate and sometimes subject to it. For the processions of beings leave no void, even less so than do the positions of bodies.[95] On the contrary, everywhere there are intermediate natures between the extremes, which provide their connection with one another.

21. Not only Plato but also the Oracles have revealed this to us clearly. First they have exhorted those divine men[96] who were deemed worthy to become hearers of those mystic words: *do not gaze at nature; its name is fate*;[97] and again: *do not aid in increasing fate, whose end is <the fatal day>*;[98] and on all occasions they turn us away from a life following fate and from being governed, as they say, together with the 'fated herds'.[99] These Oracles remove us from sense perceptions and material desires. For through these we are rendered bodily and, when rendered corporeal, we are necessarily led by fate. For similarity everywhere connects beings with one another; and that which is assimilated enjoys the same regime as that to which it is assimilated, and also the same leader of this regime. For there is nothing in the universe without a leader and nothing without a principle, no matter whether you speak of wholes or parts: some parts are dominated by others, for some live this way, others another way. Next, the Oracles teach us about the most divine life and the immaculate regime, namely how those may finally be liberated from every regime of fate, who *understand the works of the father and*, as they say, *escape the ruthless fatal wing of Moira.*[100]

22. When the soul accomplishes this or a similar kind of life, it will not be among those led by fate. If, however, it wishes to 'shape bodies'[101] and to cling to the so-called corporeal goods and pursue honours and power and riches, then it suffers the same as the philosopher who embarks on a boat and is fastened to it.[102] He too is slave when the winds move the ship, when one of the sailors kicks him and one of those who tie him up brutalises him. Let us, therefore, say farewell to those things to which we are attached and consider the strength of virtue and the fact that fate cannot do anything to us, but only to the things around us. For also the accidents that, as you mentioned, recently[103] came over us from outside, have [only] deprived us of walls and stones, my friend, and have reduced wooden beams to ashes, all of which are mortal and inflammable things,[104] and have ruined our wealth: these are external things and for this reason may fall sometimes under the power of others. But no one is so powerful as to be able to take away something of what depends on us, even if he had all human power. For if we are self-controlled, we shall remain so when all these possessions have departed, and if we love contemplation of beings, we shall not be deprived of this disposition either. And even when those most terrible losses that you mention have occurred, we for our part will go on praising the rulers of all things and investigating the causes of events.

23. We should not, then, reproach the soul for its subjection to necessity on the basis of its lowest activities, but start from its superior activities to admire its 'virtue without a master'.[105] And if we think in this way, nothing will disturb us when the inferior parts suffer. But when our body is disturbed and we say that *we* are suffering terribly, it is not we who say this, but it is an utterance of desire; for the pleasures of the body belong to desire, hence also pains. And when we suffer from being deprived of our riches or not obtaining riches, [it is again not *we* who suffer, but the desirous soul]; for also the love of money[106] belongs to this soul. And again, when we are angry because we have been dishonoured and fallen out of power, this is not a passion of the higher soul, but of the soul that is seated around the heart.[107] For the love of honour belongs to that part. If reason in us is deceived by all such passions, it follows the inferior parts, and surrenders together with them, being a blind intellect and not yet having purified the principle by which it can see itself and what is before itself and after itself. But having been made pure of those things in which it was clothed[108] when it fell down, it will know where to find that which depends on it and how it is not to be found in corporeal things – for these come after it – nor in those beings wherein one would put self-determination[109] – for these are before it – but in living according to virtue. For virtue alone is free and 'without a master' and 'fitting for a free man',[110] truly the power of the soul, and he who possesses it is a master. For it is the function of every power to contain and preserve its subject.

24. If, then, someone were to look at vice of the soul, he will be looking at weakness, even if the soul has all other power.[111] There is indeed a distinction between the power of the instruments and that of those who are to use the instruments.[112] Every soul, then, has a share in the state of freedom insofar as it has a share of virtue. And insofar as it has a share of vice and weakness, it also has a share in the state of being enslaved to others, and not only to fate, but, so to speak, to all those factors that are capable of giving the object of their desire to those who want it, or are capable of taking it away. Since even the person who has virtue is only subservient to those capable of providing him with what he desires and increasing it together with him. These are the gods, among whom true virtue is found and from whom comes the virtue in us. And Plato too in some texts calls this willing slavery the greatest freedom.[113] For by serving those who have power over all, we become similar to them, so that we also govern the whole world.[114] As Plato says, 'when the soul is perfect and winged, it journeys on high and governs the whole world'.[115] This is the privilege of the most divine among our souls, just as it belongs to inferior souls to be impeded by the body as by a prison, and to live an involuntary life instead of a voluntary and free life, whereas it is proper to those souls that are intermediary, insofar as they are liberated from passions and bodies, to ascend above necessity to the life that has power over becoming.[116]

25. Further, if the intellect and god are prior to the soul and after the soul come affections and bodies, and if it is a property of the latter to act in a necessitated manner and of the intellect and god to act in a manner superior to all necessity and to be solely free, then the soul [will be in different states depending upon] whether it sides with the latter or the former: it will either take on the necessity of inferior things or put forward the freedom of the superior, and it will be subservient, either ruled from above or from below, and, while a slave, will either reign together with its masters or be a slave together with those who are only slaves. Thus when the soul in this world rises up and resumes its power, namely virtue, it will consider nothing terrible, whatever may happen to the body and goods external to the body. For the affections of the organs are not transmitted to their users, but, no matter what condition the organs are in, the person will act according to virtue. If his body happens to be sick, he will be courageous; if it happens to be healthy, he will be moderate; when confronted with poverty, he will act with magnanimity; when endowed with riches, he will act with magnificence, everywhere setting over the [external] goods that seem to flow abundantly the virtue that will use them, and opposing to adversities the virtue that frees one from slavery; and with internal strength he escapes, warding off the blows from without. For you should not think that the often quoted words 'to move with a given force a given weight'[117] applies only to you [engineers]: it applies even more to those who live according to virtue to adorn the power given from the universe with another power that is truly a power. The person with this disposition is noble and free, whereas the evil person is a slave to all things, even if he reigns over all things. He is in a similar condition to those people in Egypt, who had to put on laughing masks when being punished.[118] Necessity has power over these people, as they are incapable of dominating themselves. Since they are estranged from the gods, the universe uses them as if they were irrational beings.[119]

26. When, then, you want to see what depends on us, look at the soul that lives in accordance with nature. The soul that lives in accordance with nature is that which is not infirm.[120] For nothing in a natural state is infirm. Now the soul that is not filled with evil is not infirm, for evil is what is infirm in all things. And if you look in this way, you will see the nature of what depends on us and how it uses all circumstances in the right way, either preventing the affections of the inferior parts from coming about or curing them if they come about, leaving it to fate to act upon that which comes after the soul, the realm over which fate is master, whereas the soul is connected 'with the beings prior to it, from which it is not cut off, since they are superior'.[121]

So much for our second investigation.

3. Different modes of knowledge

27. But let us next proceed to the third discussion and give an account of the different modes of knowledge.[122] If we do not distinguish them, we shall not notice our errors both in regard to reality and to the doctrines of the divine Plato.[123] Well then, among the [many] kinds of knowledge discussed by Aristotle and also by Plato, we shall consider [first] the knowledge that only grasps the truth of the fact without its cause, which they call opinion (*doxa*).[124] They usually assign it as first knowledge to the souls in the process of purification, both to those being educated in regard to practical matters and to those already set free from human affairs and 'occupied with beings'.[125] For education is a purification of the immoderation in the passions, and far more, a path from moderation of the passions (*metriopatheia*) towards the absence of passions (*apatheia*),[126] when reason no longer desires to suffer together with passion, albeit in moderation, but shakes off the whole scenery of the passions.[127]

28. Such being this knowledge, the philosophers 'from the same school', as is said,[128] have transmitted to us another form of knowledge leading upwards, namely that which proceeds from principles taken as suppositions and which knows causes and draws necessary conclusions in all cases. They found out that arithmetic and geometry are such a kind of knowledge.[129] Because those sciences argue and conclude from necessary premises, they take precedence over knowledge based purely on opinion; but because they stop at their own principles and leave, above them, the principles of these without bothering about them, they show that they fall short of the most perfect knowledge.[130] As he [sc. Aristotle] says, 'the geometer will not argue against someone who abolishes his principles'.[131] Hence, whatever follows from the principles admitted in these sciences will be evident, but whatever concerns the principles themselves will be left aside as being unclear and unknown.

29. Ascending higher, 'allow me to speak of a third'[132] form of knowledge of the human soul, that which ascends 'through all' the forms, so to say, towards the One and 'unconditional' principle, dividing some, analysing others, 'making the one multiple' and 'the multiple one'.[133] This knowledge Socrates defines in the *Republic* as the 'coping-stone' of the mathematical sciences, and the stranger in the *Epinomis* calls it the 'interconnection' of the sciences.[134] For it is from this science that the geometer and each of the other scientists will draw knowledge of their own principles, because it connects the many and divided principles with the one principle of all things. For what this principle is in all beings, this is in geometry the point, in arithmetic the unit, and in each of the other sciences that which is the most simple; for from there each of the sciences brings forth and demonstrates its own object.[135] But each of these principles is called and is a particular principle, whereas the principle of all beings is a principle in an absolute sense and it is to this that the supreme science ascends.

30. The fourth kind of knowledge you need to understand is even simpler than the latter, as it no longer uses methods such as analysis or synthesis or division or demonstration,[136] but contemplates beings by means of simple intuitions, as it were with immediate vision (*autoptic*).[137] Those capable of such activity praise it, calling it with reverence 'intellect', and no longer 'science'. Or have you not heard that Aristotle in his books on demonstration says something like this, namely that the intellect in us is superior to all science, and that he defines it as 'that by which we know the terms'?[138] And that Plato in the *Timaeus* declares that intellect and science are forms of knowledge of the soul concerning beings?[139] For science seems to belong to the soul, insofar as the soul is knowledge, whereas the intellect belongs to it, insofar as the soul is an image of what truly is intellect. This is because the latter sees the intelligible forms, or rather is those forms, in one intuition, as [someone] says,[140] and contact with the objects known. Thus it contemplates both itself as thinking and the forms as existing in itself. Hence, it thinks what they are and at the same time thinks that it is thinking, knowing also what it is itself. Imitating this intellect as far as possible, the soul itself also becomes intellect, transcending science and abandoning the many procedures in the course of which it was 'first embellished',[141] and raising its eye only towards beings, it thinks the things by coming into touch[142] with them in the same way as the intellect. But the soul comes into touch with different objects at different times, whereas the intellect comes into touch with them all at the same time. For 'the father of all things, he says, bestowed this fate upon it.[143]

31. After all of these, I want you to accept even a fifth meaning of 'knowledge', even though you trusted in Aristotle who only leads up to intellectual activity, but suggests nothing beyond it. But I want you to follow Plato and the theologians before Plato, who are accustomed to praise for us a knowledge beyond the intellect and who commonly call it a truly 'divine madness',[144] and to arouse what is called the 'one of the soul', and no longer our intellectual faculty, and to connect it with the

One itself.[145] For all things are known by something similar to them: the sensible by sense perception, the scientific object by science, the intelligible by the intellect, the One by what is like the One.[146] So then, when thinking, the soul knows both itself and what it thinks through 'touch', as we said, but when it is transcending thinking,[147] it knows neither itself nor that towards which it directed its own 'one'. It loves then to be quiet, having closed its eyes to thoughts that go downward, having become speechless and silent in internal silence.[148] For how else could it attach itself to the most ineffable of all things than by putting to sleep the chatter in it? Let it therefore become one, so that it may see the One, or rather not see the One.[149] For by seeing, the soul will see an intelligible object and not what is beyond intellect, and it will think something that is one, not the One itself.

32. Thus, my friend, when someone actualises what really is the most divine activity of the soul, and entrusts himself only to the 'flower of the intellect'[150] and brings himself to rest not only from the external motions, but also from the internal,[151] he will become a god as far as this is possible for a soul, and will know only in the way the gods know everything in an ineffable manner, each according to their proper one. But as long as we are concerned with the things below, we shall find it difficult to believe that, whereas the divine knows all things in an indivisible and supereternal manner, beings are eternally what they are, whereas things that come to be happen in time; and yet there is neither time nor eternity in the One.

These, then, are the different kinds of knowledge in us. With these in mind it is possible to solve the problems about whether the soul here below can know or not know the truth.

Part II. Solution of the problems raised by Theodore

Having carried out the three examinations that we said were necessary [preambles to] the articulation[152] of what we are investigating, we shall now turn to the problems themselves and I shall adduce for each of them the corresponding solutions.

1. Refusal of responsibility for failures

33. First you write – as if it were a sufficient argument for holding that *the notion of what depends on us is nonsense and that only the causality of the celestial Moirai*[153] *prevail in all that happens* – the following: *We human beings consider ourselves responsible for the outcome, whenever we do the right thing, but whenever we fail, we transfer the responsibility to that [celestial] cause rather than to our choice.* By discussing this difficulty you believe that the common notion about fate comes to the fore, namely that it exists and plays a more important role in human actions than our own impulses.[154]

34. I too do not see human beings acting otherwise: they attribute responsibility for their successes to themselves, for their failures to others. But we differ in the following respect. You believe that the opinion of the masses is sufficient as a judgement about reality, whereas I believe that they reason as they do because of some evil and irrational self-love.[155] However, truly wise people, for whom it is appropriate to look at the whole and the parts and not to overlook how the parts are ordered to the whole, make the god from whom comes the good for all, the primordial cause of all that happens. After him, they posit as cause the periodic revolution of the world and the appropriate time, in which the events are adjusted and ordered to the whole, whereby there is nothing episodic in the government of the whole.[156] They consider themselves to be a third cause whenever they obtain something after making choices and contribute by their own impulses to the accomplishment of what is to be done. But whenever something occurs contrary to their choice, only then do they rightly impute the responsibility to the whole and to its action as being overwhelming. This is because particular things must everywhere act together with the whole, whereas the whole can act both with and without the particulars. This is the way wise people divide up actions and not as you have done. Listen to what Plato exclaims in the *Laws*: 'God governs all human affairs, and together with god fortune and the decisive moment (*kairos*);[157] yet a more amenable factor should come as third after these, skill'.[158] 'For at the decisive moment of a tempest the navigator's skill' also makes some contribution, as does the art of medicine to restoring health, and, in general, politics in the case of practical actions. Therefore, even if we succeed, we must attribute responsibility to the decisive moment of fate[159] and to god, in order that what happens may have three causes.[160] The first is that which makes it good, the second that which makes it fixed into a single conformity with the universe, the third is the purely human factor. For every human deed is a part of the universe, but not *vice versa*. For also the other living beings, which are parts of the universe, must both act and suffer. And every part of this cosmic system and drama has the good as its end.[161] No part is relinquished without ordination; rather, it is woven together for the well-being of the universe. However, the reverse does not hold: not everything that obtains the good is co-ordinated with the cosmic governance. There is also a life above the world, namely the life of the gods and that of the souls that dance above fate and follow providence.[162]

35. Where, then, must we situate in this context that which depends on us, when what happens is connected with the periodic revolution of the world, or again, when it comes about due to that cause alone? Where else, then, shall we say, but in our own interior choices and impulses? We ourselves are masters only of these, whereas we share control over external events with many other causes, which are more powerful. This is because what happens outside ourselves must take place as a part of the universe in order for it to happen at all. It happens when the universe joins in assenting to it and collaborates with it, so that the universe may act upon itself, acting with a part of itself on another and undergoing influence from another part. And for these reasons, in regard to events, we praise some people and blame others, as if they were masters of these events through their choice. And however we may qualify the events that take place, we do not say that the universe has this [moral] character, but the person who acts. This is because the [moral] quality in what happens did not come from the world, but from the life of the acting person.[163] He is co-ordinated with the universe because of the universe and he is in turn of such and such quality because he is a part. That what we write is true, the oracles too will show you. For they often give victory to our choices and not merely to the order of the cosmic revolutions, for example, when they say 'look at yourself and clothe yourself' or again 'know yourself'; and other oracles say 'believe that you are outside the body and you will be'.[164] And what else should we say, when it is even said that diseases spring forth in us voluntarily, arising from the type of life we lead.[165]

36. Therefore, one must not refer all events only to the order in the universe, as we neither attribute them all to our impulses, nor again deprive the soul of the power of choice, since it has its very being precisely in this, in choosing, avoiding this, running after that, even though, as regards events, our choice is not master of the universe.[166] For one must require of every cause only as much as it is capable of. However, the faculty that depends on us is not only a capacity for acting but also a capacity of choice, choosing to act <either> on itself or together with other factors. And it is because of its choice that we say that it makes failures and acts rightly, since even if the result is good, but the agent acts on the basis of an evil choice, we say that the action is bad. For, what is good in what is done is due to a [favourable] external factor, but what is bad is due to the choice of the agent. Thus it is evident to all that we are masters of our actions to the extent that they are deliberately chosen.[167]

2. The argument from divination

37. After this inquiry you go on to say: *all human beings are in all circumstances curious to know about the future, even in matters that seem to depend on us.*[168] This, you write, is yet another indication that we are not master of anything, since we do not know what will happen. This is shown by our interest in divination even in matters where we ourselves make a choice. Hence you conclude, in short: *if we are all lovers of divination,*[169] *nothing depends on us.*

But in defence I will reverse your argument. If nothing depends on us and events are brought about necessarily by the celestial movement,[170] then we would not be lovers of divination. For what would be the use of divination in regard to events necessitated from elsewhere? Whether we know that they will take place or will not take place, this knowledge is superfluous, since both are necessary. For it is impossible that what is necessary will not happen, even if we foresee it and deliberate in advance about it a thousand times. If, then, we are not concerned in vain about the future – and we cannot be so in vain, since this concern is natural to us, and nothing natural occurs in vain[171] – we should not make all things necessary by connecting them to the [celestial] revolution, but admit that foreknowledge also has some utility for our lives, not in order that we merely undergo [events] with foreknowledge, but in order that by our foreknowledge we may become more prepared to co-operate ourselves somehow with the future events or not to co-operate.

38. Besides, not only rites of divination, but also prayers[172] and all the rituals of the priests contribute to these events, people say. Or should we send away and banish the priests having 'anointed them with myrrh and crowned them'?[173] And shall we not allow people to raise their hands nor allow supplications addressed to those who can repulse the celestial influences?[174] In vain, then, all human beings 'always invoke a god'[175] in difficult circumstances in which they have hope, and Apollo himself announced in vain in his oracle that it is possible for those who do these things to escape the punishment that depends on the heavenly cycles, whereas those who fail to do so will inevitably meet with terrible [vengeance].[176] Yet if it did not depend on them to do something or not to do it, how would it not be utterly absurd to make such distinctions and to ascribe what follows from the oracles to their choices? But we should not inveigh against god nor should we do away with the utility of divination and theurgy from human lives, for you have all those reports, both from Greeks and non-Greeks, as evidence that, because of divination, deriving either from divine inspiration or from human art,[177] many people have often known what they had to do, and knowing it have freed themselves from inexorable evils in the future. All these stories are readily available for you to read.

39. For the present investigation the following argument is, in my view, appropriate. In some cases we say that the celebrated mantic and the rituals of the priests have a place in whether something happens or not, in other cases we say that they are dominated by what comes forth from the universe. Thus, when all the divine and demonic causes in the universe contribute to one effect and speak as it were in one voice, then also the theurgical works seem to be ineffective – for it is impossible for a part to oppose the whole and to perform contrary actions – and the foreknowledge does not add or remove something of the events that have been predicted. But whenever, in a situation where there are many agents, some bring forth one thing and some another, for instance, some bring forth corruption and others a cure for those who are ill – in every story there are reports of such effects of the celestial bodies on us – then the application of theurgy may dissolve the influxes that come down from harmful agents, using as co-operative powers the influxes of the agents that are beneficial to us,[178] and the examination of the future plays an important role in the effects. In short, in this situation, the faculty that depends on us is lined up either with one set of causes or with another and it weighs down, as in a balance,[179] by its own movement, sometimes towards this end, sometimes towards another.

What I am writing, is of external events. But in all cases this again, I say, must be the presupposition that an impetus and a choice of a certain type characterises that which depends on us and that it is the work of a soul that remains in it [the soul] and does not go out into the universe.

3. One vital force permeating the universe

40. The next point you raise, seems to me to be the following.[180] <In your view one vital force> *governs all living beings and we ourselves and all other animals receive, in a descending scale, life given from the ether and from the first revolution [of the heaven]. In the brain it is rational life; in the sense organs this same life is implanted with regard to diverse sensible objects and is called perception: sight or hearing or one of the other senses. For life is differentiated by its substrates, but it is one and undifferentiated in itself.*

41. Having heard you set out these matters, I was surprised to observe that you, though a lover of philosophy and of intellectual speculations – and why do I mention [only] intellectual speculations? For you are also versed in mathematical learning[181] and in the discoveries of geometry and arithmetic, – attribute so much importance to sense perceptions. You call these perceptions not dim images of our rational and intellectual essence, which 'barely' grasp the objects of knowledge 'through dim organs',[182] but consider them to be this very intellectual essence, having become, in a descending scale, distinguished from it and from each other only by the different properties of the organs.

Yet, as we have demonstrated somewhere before,[183] all sense perception is inseparable from body and incapable of reflecting upon itself, whereas our rational and intellectual life has the capacity to know itself and to reflect upon itself through self-knowledge. For every cognitive principle in act is reflected upon the object of its knowledge, just as what belongs to oneself is reflected upon oneself. What kind of identity, then, do you see between the sensitive soul and the intellectual soul? Between that which looks down and that which reaches up to the principles of all things, between that which is buried in bodies[184] and that which is purified from bodies in its natural activities, between that which can never know the truth and that which always yearns for being and sometimes attains the truth, if its natural desire is not in vain nor related to something else.

42. It goes without saying that it is absurd – if one may call the impossible absurd – to let the essence of the divine soul emanate from the ether. For all things that have come from the ether have come into being as bodies, whereas the Athenian stranger demonstrates that the soul is 'older than all bodies'.[185] If, however, you do not conceive the ether as a body but as an ethereal intellect or an intellectual soul that causes the ether to revolve,[186] even then, it seems to me, you do not discover the truest cause of the soul. For the source of souls, from which the ethereal soul, the souls of the sublunary elements and the souls of the demons proceed, is something different. We too must focus on that source which, Plato, in my view, concealing the truth, calls a 'mixing bowl (*crater*)'. According to Plato's account, the demiurge did not mix the soul from ether, but mixed it somehow there before the bodies, where, as Timaeus says, 'he had also blended and mixed the soul of the universe'.[187] The Oracles revealed by the gods also celebrate the crater as the source in itself of all kinds of soul, empyreal, ethereal, material,[188] and this source they make depend on the whole life-giving goddess;[189] and attaching to this goddess the whole of fate, they draw up two series, the psychic and that which we are accustomed to call fatal; and making the soul derive from the first series, they say that it is enslaved to fate whenever, becoming irrational, it changes master, exchanging providence for fate.[190]

43. By placing our soul on the same level as the senses you declared it, as I said,[191] unworthy of geometry and arithmetic, not to speak of intellectual activity. You may come to understand this if you consider that it is precisely the first task of these sciences[192] to stop the soul from acting with the senses and lead it away from these, as far as possible, and accustom it to look inside[193] itself and see immaterial reasons, and to investigate demonstrations that are in conflict with the senses. For the senses do not admit what is indivisible, whereas the sciences teach us that divisible things have their existence from those that are indivisible; and divisible things are the starting-point for the former, whereas indivisible things for the latter. Further, the senses are supposed to know the fact that there is something as well as its singular aspects,[194] the sciences that which is universal and that which always has the same nature, which they could not acquire from the sense objects – for imperfect objects cannot be the cause of that which is perfect,[195] – but receive from above, from the intellect. Therefore, they judge over the senses and reproach them for the inaccuracy of their knowledge, for grasping the objects together with affections, for the indeterminate movements from the sense objects. In fact, the cognitions of the senses are really playing, whereas those of the sciences are already serious and accustom us to keep away from playthings and to hunt for real instead of playful knowledge.[196]

44. Therefore, this (sensible) life must be ruled by fate and undergo different influences at different times together with the bodies, in which that which depends on fate is situated. For every form [of life] that is inseparable from matter comes forth from this source and is maintained in existence by it. [Such a life] is not able to reflect upon itself and to distinguish between the affection that comes upon it from outside and the true reality, but merely expresses that which the affection announced. Therefore, this life is one of the things that are extrinsically moved, since it does not have an activity that is free from such things. But the other kind of life must be intellectual according to its nature and it cannot bear to follow the 'violent affections'[197] of sense perception. It contains in itself the criteria[198] for discerning deceitful motions from outside; it adds that which is lacking in that which sense perception experiences and refutes what is untrue in them, and it does all this from within.[199] For perception cannot be judged with the data of perception, but only with intellectual reasons, which sense perception is unable to receive. In fact, the intellectual life must be opposed to sense perception, as it is immaterial, separate and self activating.[200] To this life we must attribute choice, which may tend to both sides, upwards and downwards, towards the intellect from which it originated and towards sense perception which it generated.[201] Sense perception, however, and all forms of life together with the bodies are without choice, as are also the bodies. Since the rational soul is intermediary between intellect and sense perception, it is moved in both directions because of the unstable inclination of its choice; it becomes relationally either of the extremes, although it is neither of them essentially.[202] That the soul is intermediary is clear since it receives perfection from the intellect and deceit from sense perception.[203]

This may suffice, I believe, as a correction of your views.

4. Intermezzo: hedonism

45. I now turn to your opinion about the good, which you have put forward in the middle of your arguments. You claim that *the good is what is pleasurable to each individual, and that it is so by convention:*[204] *for different customs prevail among different people.* I would certainly be ashamed myself to discuss this view, if I were not writing frankly what I believe to a man who is my friend, for an opinion on these matters is unworthy, I think, of my philosophical conviction and of my age.[205]

That a young man should entertain such an opinion would not surprise me, since youth in most cases 'pays attention to what people think'.[206] But for someone who has made the older 'intellect leader'[207] intellectual thoughts of a prudent judgement are fitting, I believe, and not the views that the masses with their unstable impulses shout. For it is not because the Persians have other views on what is pleasurable and what is lawful corresponding to what they like, and the Greeks have other views about the same practices and other peoples yet other views, that the good itself is something relative, just as the pleasurable appears different to different people. For of all things the good surely is the only one that can be said to be by nature and is indeed by nature.[208] Whoever obtains what is by nature good for everyone will have the goal that is fitting for man. But whoever fails to reach it, even if he gains a thousand pleasures from the apparent goods that are available to him, 'culls the imperfect fruit'[209] of such pleasure.

46. But, as it appears, it was true that 'given one absurdity, others follow'.[210] This is what happens to you, I believe. For having made fate superior to soul, you have ranked the soul together with the irrational perceptions; and having concluded that they are the same thing, you have made the good and the pleasurable one.

One should remove from the soul both the former and the latter view. Otherwise we may find ourselves, without noticing it, attributing to human beings nothing different to what we grant to irrational animals, whose life cannot reflect upon itself, whose nature is inclined towards the earth,[211] whose knowledge is mixed with material affections. Yet Plato has established, so to speak, 'with adamantine arguments'[212] that the good and the pleasurable are not identical, not even if all cattle vote for this view.[213] For we must not be emulators of cattle but of the gods, among whom intellect holds sway and the genuine good, which is more divine than the intellect itself. Since all this has been demonstrated in the *Gorgias*, the *Philebus* and the *Republic*,[214] I consider it superfluous to 'report again' in this writing 'what has been clearly said'.[215]

47. Yet I shall add the following to what has been said. One should not entrust the search for the good to enjoyment[216] lest the spell of pleasure put us out of our mind. Rather, one should explain the manifold differences in human customs and practices by referring to the different lives of souls: the rational, the irascible, the appetitive.[217] For these customs sprout from these lives: 'not from an oak or from a rock', as it is said.[218] But the 'many-headed beast' has persuaded some people to take on customs such as those of the Persians, the 'lion-like' part of the soul has made other people go for the way of life of the Thracians, whereas yet other people are ruled by reason in what is lawful and what is truly good.[219] But whereas what is pleasurable is common to all – since for everyone what is desirable is pleasurable when it is present – the good is not shared by all but only by those in whom reason takes the lead. For the passions do not see the good, but reason alone does so. And whereas for reason the pleasurable and the good are the same, creation has not entrusted to the blind passions 'the hunt for the good, but for the pleasurable'.[220] For every type of life experiences pleasure whenever its activity is not impeded.[221] Hence, customs are manifold and what is pleasurable is diverse and different for different people, but what is good is found only among those people in whom reason dominates the passions. For we should not give authority to desire, lest we come to the same state as donkeys, nor to the irascible, lest we become like lions, but to that part in us that is 'most excellent' and that we are only or 'most of all'.[222] For although we are all composed of many parts, better and worse, we have our being according to the best part. For the nature of the universe aims at what is best.

5. Scepticism

48. But what is the problem you raise next in your letter?[223] It seems to me that – *having heard Socrates say in many passages (1) that he knows nothing and having him heard laugh at those who claim to know everything*[224] *and (2) contend that 'we shall know the truth'* [225] *fully when we depart from this world and (3) argue that even the more accurate sciences are not really sciences*[226] – *you doubt whether it is altogether possible to know the truth or whether we are only 'dreaming'*[227] *about it*.

Yet you should have realised that if we cannot know the truth, we also cannot know whether what depends on us exists or not. For ignorance prevents us equally from taking a position for the one or the other alternative. How, then, can we use the fact that we do not know the truth to demonstrate the non-existence of what depends on us, when ignorance has the same power, or rather lack of power, to show both that this faculty exists and that it does not?

49. That we may not fall into such a trap, we have first distinguished all forms of knowledge,[228] both those which the soul can have in this world and those which it can have when it has achieved its supreme condition.[229] The former Socrates has, the latter he hopes to acquire when released from the body: moving 'over there', he says, 'he will know the truth'.[230] For the fact that there are different modes of knowledge provided him the occasion for such hope. Indeed, this too is a problem the Platonists thought worth considering, namely whether it is possible for the soul, while carrying around this thick bond,[231] to live not only by way of purification, but also in contemplation, and this problem, I think, has received reasonable investigation.[232] It is, indeed, possible for someone to contemplate even when staying in this world, as does the chorus leader in the *Theaetetus*, who is 'contemplating the stars above heaven' and 'investigating thoroughly the whole nature of beings',[233] and also the guardians in the *Republic*, who ascend towards the Good through the famous dialectic, which Plato set up as the 'cornerstone of the sciences'.[234] But it is impossible for someone to become perfectly contemplative for the reasons he explains in the *Phaedo*, namely that 'the lack of leisure' and the annoyances of the body[235] do not allow that activity to occur in us without hindrance and disturbance. For 'contemplative' is the name of a way of life, whereas 'contemplation' is the name of an activity, even if it is a single.[236]

50. Moreover, when Socrates urges us not to call the mathematical sciences precisely 'sciences',[237] he does not say this as if he denied somehow that they possess the necessity of demonstrations, but because he holds that they fall short of the supreme science, that is — why not speak plainly? — dialectic, which no longer posits as its principle the point or the monad itself but the good itself and investigates the principles of all things. This is the reason, I believe, why he assigns to mathematical objects the second section in the division of the line, whereas he assigns the section above them to the absolutely immaterial and separate forms; and to the former objects he attributed the knowledge that starts 'from a hypothesis,' and to the latter 'unconditional' knowledge.[238] The author of the *Epinomis* — a long time ago we examined this work and judged it to be inauthentic[239] — calls dialectic the 'interconnection' of the mathematical sciences,[240] since it unifies the principles of all those sciences and relates them to the one principle of all beings.

51. To be sure, Socrates is ready to say that 'he knows nothing', and the oracle of the Pythia proclaimed him for that reason to be 'the wisest of all', as he himself explains the oracle.[241] Yet you should consider the depth of what both the god and Socrates said. For he did not say that merely the fact of knowing nothing is a special privilege, but rather, when one does not know, to know that one does not know. This ignorance seems to be of great utility for those who intend to become wise; in reality, however, it tends to be the same as wisdom, and the person who knows himself to be really not knowing and who is not ignorant about what he does not know, is really wise. For who else could know the one who does not know than the person who also knows the one who knows? For he must know perfectly also what he does not know, if indeed he is to know that he does not know. For if he were not to know that [i.e. what he does not know], he also would not know it if he knew it. Hence, no one could know himself perfectly as not knowing before he had known himself as knowing. For, then, he will notice at the same time both what he knows and what he does not know, and he will understand both that he knows and that he does not know, having a form of knowledge intermediary between that which only knows and that which does not know at all, that is, on the one hand the intellect, on the other sense perception. For the latter does not know the truth at all, since it does not even know the very essence of the sensible things, of which it pretends to be knowledge. The former [i.e. the intellect] knows immediately the very essence of a being and the truth itself, as it really is. Intermediary between them is the soul: it knows the essences of beings, insofar as it exists before sense perception, and does not know them, insofar as it comes after the intellect.[242] When, then, someone has become wise, he will know <himself> both knowing that he knows and knowing that he does not know. So far, then, my friend, the appropriate interpretation of what Socrates and the oracle say about true wisdom.

52. Thus, it is not because Socrates separates the mathematical sciences from the first science [i.e. dialectic], not because he expresses his hope of obtaining true knowledge after his departure from this world, nor because of the oracle of Pythia that we should discredit scientific reasoning. For it is Plato himself who claims that anyone who 'abolishes science could not assert anything about whatsoever'.[243] But what sort of knowledge the soul could acquire when it is still with the body and what sort after having been released from this bond, <has been established before>.[244] And that some forms of knowledge are both science and not science, and that there is one true science and an intellect superior to science and a deifying intuition superior to intellect.[245] It is this knowledge which the soul envisages and being unable to acquire it in this life, it desires to depart from the body, hoping to gain a supernatural and divine apprehension of all beings. But enough has been said about these matters.

6. Misfortune of good people

53. Next you raise the following problem: *why do good people fare badly, failing to achieve the goals they have set, whereas bad people achieve what they desire.* You – at any rate – think *this too is evidence that there is no such a thing as what depends on us.*[246]

Yet, it is possible to ward off this problem by expressing it differently: if the fact that things do not always happen for good people as they want them to[247] were evidence of the non-existence of that which depends on us, then the fact that things happen for bad people in accordance with their wishes would also be an indication that it exists. But it may be better not to attack your argument polemically, but to demonstrate to you just this point: to my knowledge, none of the ancient philosophers has ever put forward this problem to eliminate that which depends on us, but rather to examine providence. The famous Plotinus, Iamblichus, and your namesake [sc. Theodore of Asine], struggled relentlessly with this problem.[248] In fact, the unexpected outcome of fortuitous events may really shake up the preconceptions about providence which we have, without having been taught, and the treatment [of this difficulty] requires thoughtful investigation, if someone, after having been healed[249] of this problem, is to attribute everything to providence.

54. I know, as I have said, that this problem was raised by our predecessors not to eliminate what depends on us, but rather to examine providence. That this problem, far from being an argument of the non-existence of what depends on us, is rather an argument for its existence, we may come to understand when we consider the following. If we were not master of anything, if we had of ourselves no life of free choice, if good and evil did not come from us, but were produced from elsewhere, then it would no longer make sense to raise problems about the outcome of events, which are good or evil from external causes, on the basis that they occur contrary to merit. For if human beings could not make themselves good and bad, it would not be necessary to recompense both the good and the bad for their respective way of living, nor would anything whatever be due to those who are not responsible for the life they have. Hence, if, [as they pretend], recompense with the goods of fortune is contrary to merit, they must surely themselves be responsible for the lives for which they wish to obtain what they deserve in the distribution of goods from the universe. For also in the case of all our external goods, we do not require that there are recompenses in the things we receive from the universe, but in those goods we somehow collaborate in.[250] If, then, what depends on us does not exist, we do not have anything from ourselves; but if this is the case, we also should not require recompenses in things that come to us from elsewhere; and if so, we also should not complain about the distribution of outcomes contrary to merit.

55. If, then, what depends on us does not exist, one should no [longer] examine how it is possible that, contrary to merit, good people fail to achieve their goals, whereas bad people achieve them. But assuming that what depends on us does exist and that providence dominates all things, we shall try to persuade you, after having used force, by the following argument.[251] How's that? Did we not agree that what depends on us is not a force ruling over external events, but only collaborating with them?[252] If so, it is reasonable that it arranges what is internal according to its power, but not what is external, since it also needs other factors not within its power to dispose those things. I myself, when I consider these problems, have great admiration for the noble Epictetus[253] who often exhorts us not to confuse what depends on us with what does not depend on us, and not to be in such a state with regard to things that do not depend on us so as to believe they ought absolutely to occur. Otherwise we shall bear with difficulty when they do not occur. But since those effects are due to follow from what depends on us, there arises a problem, when they do not follow, since we also take as good what is not good and seek to obtain it. It would be better to search always for what really depends on us and to purchase it for ourselves and to abandon what is external and does not depend on us to the forces that produce it, since these are masters of them and know what they do, and to prepare us for all things that do not depend on us through what depends on us.

Through these arguments we have explained the problem insofar as it concerns what depends on us. But, as we have seen, one could say much more about this problem with regard to the doctrine of providence. Much has been said about it by the ancient men I mentioned, who also solve the problem in this sense.[254]

7. Real freedom is a divine privilege

56. Next you ask *what is this faculty that depends on us*,[255] – a question you had better put at the beginning of your arguments, and then raised problems about it. After investigation you define it as *that which is by nothing dominated or mastered, but is*, as you literally say, *self-determined (autoperigraptos) and self-activated (autoenergêtos)*.[256] *But if it is of such a nature, it is also absolutely incorruptible and supremely powerful and it belongs only to the first lord of all beings*,[257] *whereas what depends on us is no longer a characteristic of us.*

57. This definition is far from the concept of 'what depends on us' that the ancient philosophers had in mind when they assigned this faculty to human souls. That is my thesis, but it is up to you to check whether what I say is true.

The ancients always take the expression 'what depends on us' as referring to the activity of choice, making us masters of choosing and avoiding either some good or its opposite. For they do not identify choice (*proairesis*) and will (*boulêsis*): the will, they say, only regards the good, whereas choice is likewise of good and not good things, just as opinion (*dokêsis*)[258] is also of what is not good. Therefore, choice characterises the soul, since choice is equally open to both, and it is appropriate to the intermediate nature which is moved towards both. Our ordinary way of speaking also bears witness to this: for we praise the choices of some people and blame those of others.[259] Evil, however, we say, is wanted (*abouleuton*) by nobody, and to those who choose it, evil seems to be a good. For no soul would knowingly choose evil, but would avoid it.[260] Due to ignorance, however, [the soul] is occupied with it. For although it has by nature a 'keen love' of the good, it is unable to see where the good lies.[261] Hence, because the soul has in its own being this ambivalent inclination, I mean towards good and evil, philosophers have called this faculty of the soul through which we are able to choose one thing over another, the 'elective' (*proairetikon*).

58. With the method of division you can also arrive at the following definition of this faculty. Every faculty is either rational or irrational. Choice must also be situated in one of these. But it is not irrational; for we all agree that irrational beings live without choice;[262] hence it must be a rational faculty. Now, every rational faculty is either cognitive or appetitive, as is also every irrational faculty. If choice is that which it is said to be, i.e., choice and desire, it must be some appetite.[263] Now, every appetite either regards only that which is truly good or only that which is seemingly good or both. We cannot say that choice regards only what is truly good – for otherwise it would never be right to criticise it – or only the apparent good – for otherwise it would not deserve frequent praise; hence it is a faculty related to both.

59. To sum up, choice is a rational appetitive faculty that strives for some good, either true or apparent, and leads the soul towards both. Through this faculty the soul ascends and descends, does wrong and does right. Considering the activity of this faculty authors have called its ambivalent inclination 'the crossroad' in us.[264] Hence the elective faculty and 'what depends on us' seem to be identical. Due to this faculty we differ both from divine and from mortal beings, since neither of them is subject to this ambivalent inclination: divine beings, because of their excellence, are established only among true goods, and mortal beings, because of their deficiency, only among apparent goods. The intellect characterises the former, sense perception the latter; and 'the intellect is our king, sense perception our messenger'.[265]

60. We are in the middle, having been fixed in the faculty of choice and we are capable of moving in one direction or in another,[266] but wherever we move, we are dominated by the universal causes and receive what we deserve; if we move towards the better, we act as intellect, if towards the inferior, as perception. Therefore, 'what depends on us' does not consist in the power and licence[267] to do all things. For the power that exercises authority over all things is unitary; and therefore it is also a power over all things, since it is one and good;[268] the elective faculty is dual, and therefore not of all things, because it is, by its ambivalent inclinations, inferior to the power which comes before all things. It would have become itself the power over all things, if it had not had the impulse of choice, but had only been will. For a willed life is in accordance with the good and it makes what depends on us extremely powerful and it is really godlike: thanks to this life the soul becomes god and governs the whole world, as Plato says.[269]

61. Therefore, the faculty that depends on us belongs neither to the first order of things nor to the last, but to the middle. But you seem to have thought that the expression 'what depends on us' refers to a power that dominates all things, a power that can lead all things in accordance with its impulses and obtain whatever it desires.[270] It is not by limiting its power within the domain of desirable things inside the souls, that you have made the elective soul such as it is, but by giving it the power also over what does not depend on us. For what is outside the soul does not depend on us. Therefore, our life is a mixture of what does not depend on us and what depends on us.[271] And virtuous people have much that depends on them, for due to their virtue they also make moderate use of all things that do not depend on them, colouring[272] even those things and making them as it were in their power, insofar as they always bring order to what is presently given. In the case of the many, however, there is much more that does not depend on them; for they follow external things, not having an internal life powerful enough to assimilate those externals. Hence the virtuous are said to be free and are indeed free, because their activity depends upon them and is not the slave of what does not depend on them. The other people, however, cry out necessity, burying that which depends on them together with that which does not, and so have nothing which depends on them.

8. Colophon: divine providence excludes human freedom

62. As a culmination of all problems you added this last.[273] *You ask whether god knows what will happen with us or not. If he does not know it, he will not be different from us who do not know it either*, as you say. *But if he knows it, whatever he knows will absolutely and by necessity happen. This, however, not only removes, as it may seem, that which depends on us, but also whatever is called contingent.*[274] *And this also befalls those who do not admit that all things are necessitated,*[275] *and it has been said a thousand times so to say. And they all construe the following conditional argument: 'if god knows whatever will be, what will be will be of necessity'.*

63. But some philosophers say that it is not true that god knows all things in a determinate manner and they declare that god himself is undetermined regarding things that happen in an indeterminate way, so that they may preserve what is contingent.[276] Others, who attribute to god a determinate knowledge, admitted that there is necessity in all the things that come to be. (Those are the views of respectively the Peripatetics and the Stoics.)[277] But Plato and whoever is his friend assert both that god knows future events in a determinate manner and that they happen according to their own nature, some in a determinate manner, others in an indeterminate manner. For when effects happen in a divided manner and contrary to one another, their anticipation in the gods is only according to the superior manner. What I mean is this: effects may be either incorporeal or corporeal, but within the gods the causes of both effects are incorporeal; similarly their knowledge is incorporeal; and again effects may be intellectual or not, but within the gods they are in an intellectual manner both *qua* existence and *qua* knowledge; for they know also what is without intellect in an intellectual manner. And again from the gods come both temporal and non temporal effects, but their cause and knowledge is established within the gods in a timeless manner.[278] To conclude, since there are both determinate and indeterminate effects, the gods have foreknowledge of both according to the better state of both, I mean the determinate.

64. Further, the form of knowledge must not correspond to what the object of knowledge is, but to what the subject of knowledge is, and rightly so. For knowledge does not reside in the object but in the one who knows. Hence, knowledge is similar and homogeneous with that in which it exists, but not with that wherein it does not exist. Even if the object of knowledge is indeterminate, given the fact that the one who knows is determinate, knowledge will not be indeterminate because of the object, but will be determinate because of the knowing subject. For it is possible to know the inferior in a superior manner and the superior in an inferior manner. Therefore, since the gods are superior to all things, they anticipate all things in a superior way, that is in the manner of their own existence: in a timeless way what exists according to time, as we have said, in an incorporeal way the bodies, in an immaterial way the material things, in a determinate way what is indeterminate, in a stable way what is unstable, and in an ungenerated way what is generated.

65. Therefore, it is not true that, if the gods know the future, its outcome is by necessity fixed, but one should attribute to the future an indeterminate outcome from what is determinate, and to the gods a determinate foreknowledge of what is indeterminate. For even your astronomical table, which makes uses of wheels and pins and corporeal materials, was in your foreknowledge not present in a corporeal manner. But, there [in your mind] its representation was incorporeal and it possessed in a vital manner the account of what will be made. The clock, however, was constructed in a corporeal manner from an internal knowledge that was not such.[279] If this is the case with your production, what will you say of the foreknowledge of the gods, where we find what is ineffable and really indescribable and inexplicable for us?[280] [Will you not admit] that the manner in which the gods contain all things is different and not at all comparable to the things that are produced by them? We conclude: the gods know what depends on us in a divine and timeless manner and yet we act according to our nature. And whatever we choose is foreknown by them, not because of a determination in us, but of one in them.

Conclusion

66. Those are, my dear friend,[281] my answers to your questions. Of course, it had been possible to demonstrate the existence of that which depends on us also on itself, with arguments coming from praise and blame, from advices, exhortations, and dissuasions, from judgements, accusations, and defences, from the whole political education, from legislation, from prayers, and from ritual practices, and from philosophy itself.[282] For you know well that my teacher[283] used to say that if that which depends on us is abolished, philosophy itself is shown to be useless. For what will educate us, if there is nothing that can be educated?[284] What will be educated, if it does not depend upon us to become better? Consider those arguments again and again and if you are still in doubt, do not hesitate to write to us. For on what could it be more fitting to develop arguments than on those subjects wherein nobody can accuse us of 'babbling' when we discuss them?[285] But, please, do not introduce to me the sorites[286] and the traps from the Stoics and the whole chatter of sparrows, as they say, that come 'from the same school', I beseech you.[287]

Notes

1. *ôdinas*, literally, 'throes of childbirth', 'travail', hence, what is born from this travail. In a metaphorical sense, 'the labour of the mind and its fruits', i.e. concepts. Because of the *Theaetetus*, where Socrates is presented as midwife of the young Theodorus, the metaphor became very popular among Platonists. In Proclus alone there are about 35 instances.

2. In what follows Proclus distinguishes (1) the philosophical views on providence and fate, those of the Platonists Plotinus and Iamblichus and those of Plato himself, (2) the mythological discourse (Orphic and Hellenic theology) and (3) the revelations of the Chaldean Oracles. On those different categories of sources see the Introduction, p. 5.

3. This phrase, attributed to Heraclitus (fr. B 92), is often quoted to characterise the mythological mode of theology, cf. Plotinus II 9 [33] 18,20 and Proclus, *in Remp.* I 140,16; 166,20; *Theol. Plat.* I 4, p. 18,2; *in Parm.* I 646,19; *in Crat.* 110, p. 62,3-4.

4. cf. Plato, *Tim.* 40D where it is said that the 'children of the gods' (the divine prophets) know 'their forefathers clearly'. See Proclus, *in Remp.* II 236,5; *in Tim.* III 159,9-22 and *in Parm.* VII 512,97-8.

5. Reference to the Chaldean Oracles, which, according to Proclus, reveal the divine truth without using symbols; cf. *Theol. Plat.* I 4, p. 20,13-19 and *in Parm.* I 646,27.

6. On life as a drama performed in the cosmic theatre, see the Introduction, p. 13, and also below, ch. 34,26-30.

7. On the Stoic elements in this explanation of fate as *heimarmenê*, see the Introduction, pp. 11-14.

8. Plato, *Tim.* 30C8.

9. On this representation of the cosmos, see the Introduction, pp. 13-14.

10. Reference to *Tim.* 29A5-6 where the demiurge is called 'the best of all causes'.

11. The mixture of play and seriousness is characteristic of Plato, cf. *Polit.* 268D8; 288C9; *Phil.* 30E6; *Symp.* 197E7; cf. also Proclus, *in Eucl.* 10,2-3.

12. Literally 'hunt' (*thêra*): Proclus likes the Platonic metaphor of 'hunting' (see *Phaedo* 66A3; 66C2 and many others texts). See in this treatise also chs 6,5; 17,15; 43,18.

13. On these three distinctions and their historical antecedents, see the Introduction, pp. 15-17.

14. cf. *Theaet.* 176A.

15. Reference to the myth of *Phaedr.*: 'when the soul is burdened with wrongdoing it sheds its wings and falls to the earth' (248C8).

16. As one can learn from *Elem. Theol.* §14, p. 16,9-12: 'all that exists is either moved or unmoved (*akinêta*); and if the former, either by itself or by another, that is, either self-moved (*autokinêta*) or externally moved (*heterokinêta*); so that everything is unmoved, self-moved or externally moved'. To be moved by an external force is characteristic of corporeal bodies and of whatever resides in them (for instance, material qualities or forms in matter). See also below, ch. 10.

17. cf. *Tim.* 42A3.

18. Parmenides is mentioned here, because in his Poem he draws a distinction between the 'truth' revealed to the soul, when it ascends, and the false opinions of the mortals. On the attribute 'great' (*megas*) for Parmenides, see also *Theol. Plat.* I 9, p. 34,18; *in Parm.* I 681,8; I 689,6; V 1022,12.

19. On this metaphor, see the Philological Appendix.

20. cf. *Phaedr.* 247E2.

21. cf. *Or. Chald.* fr. 129,3 (des Places). The expression can already be found in Plotinus II 3 [52] 17,24-5.

22. See the Introduction, pp. 5-11.

23. cf. below, ch. 49 and n. 232.

24. cf. *Phaedr.* 237B7-C2 (but Proclus adapted the text replacing *boulê* with *theôria*). We find the same citation in Simplicius, *in Phys.* 75,4; Philoponus, *in DA* 43,8-10; *Proleg. Plat.* 21,2-6 (with other parallels in the note of Westerink). See also Hermias, *in Phaedr.* 50,20ff.

25. Aristotle is characterised by the attribute *daimonios*, whereas Plato is called *theios*: cf. *Theol. Plat.* I 9, p. 35,4 (with note 5 on p. 141 in the edition of Saffrey-Westerink).

26. See Aristotle, *An. Post.* 2.1, 89b24-5 and 89b34. Proclus praises Aristotle for the same reason in *in Alc.* 274,32-275,7 (see the note of Segonds on p. 434, who provides several other parallels).

27. cf. Plato, *Phil.* 16C5 and Damascius (referring to Proclus), *in Phil.* 56,2 (p. 27 with note); same phrase (but used in a general sense) in *in Remp.* II 53,10; *in Parm.* IV 954,9. On the relation between dialectic and definition, see *in Parm.* V 982,11ff. ('division gives to definition its first principles').

28. The 'common notions' (*koinai ennoiai*) are concepts all human beings share by nature, without being taught. If not perverted by the influence of a bad education or an immoral life style they provide us with correct insights in the first principles of theology, mathematics, ethics, etc. Proclus here refers to the common notions of providence and fate. This Neoplatonic doctrine is of Stoic origin (cf. *SVF* 3.228). On this doctrine see the important note by Saffrey-Westerink on *Theol. Plat.* I 25, p. 110,22-3 (note on pp. 159-61), to be complemented by the note of Segonds on *in Alc.* 104,8-10 (nn. 4-5 on p. 180).

29. For this metaphor, see above, n. 12.

30. Although Aristotle does not use the expression *koinai ennoiai*, he maintains that demonstrations start from *koina axiômata* (Aristotle, *An. Post.* 1.10, 76b11-16) or from *koinai doxai* (Aristotle, *Metaph.* 3.2, 996b26ff.; cf. the Neoplatonic commentary on this passage by Syrianus, *in Metaph.* 18,9ff. ad loc.).

31. cf. *Phaedr.* 265E1.

32. The metaphor of 'kindling a light' is again of Platonic origin; see *Tim.* 39B4: the demiurge 'kindled a light, which we call sun' (quoted in Proclus, *in Tim.* III 82,15; *De Prov.* 54,4-5). See, moreover, *Ep.* 7, 341D12 (on intellectual illumination). Proclus uses the metaphor in *in Alc.* 33,19; 182,16; *in Parm.* I 617,2; II 770,23; VI 1061,26; *De Mal.* 1,10.

33. The title *proxenos* was given to a person representing the interest of a foreign state in his own community. Generally speaking, the term could indicate a protector or patron of a group.

34. Proclus' explanation of the 'common notion' of fate, as manifested in the term we use for it (*heimarmenê*), depends in fact on a wrong etymology. Following the Stoics, it was common to understand the term *heimarmenê* (which means originally 'what is allotted'; *heimarto* is the pluperfect of *meiromai*) as the 'connected chain' (*eiromenon* deriving from *eirô*) of events. Cf. *SVF* 2.915 (*heimarmenê aitia tôn ontôn eiromenê*). Thus, Proclus *in Tim.* III 272,24ff.

35. See *Elem. Theol.* §120, p. 106,5-7: 'Providence resides primitively in the gods. For indeed, where should an activity prior to intelligence be found, if not in the principles above being? And providence, as its name (*pro-noia*) shows, is an activity prior to intelligence (*pro nou*)' (trans. Dodds, see also his commentary on p. 263). Cf. also *in Tim.* I 415,8ff.: 'providence is an activity of the good'; *De Decem Dub.* 65,10: 'primary providence is god, because he is also the first good'. Already Plotinus speaks of the 'pre-thinking' (*pronoousa*) of the One (V 3 [49] 10,44).

36. cf. Plotinus V 6 [24] 5,8-11: 'this is what thinking is, a movement towards the Good in its desire of that Good; for the desire generates thought and establishes it in being along with itself; for desire of sight is seeing. The Good itself, then, must not think anything' (trans. Armstrong). The intellect is 'much praised' because it is considered to be the first principle by some philosophers. We find the same expression in *Theol. Plat.* I 19, p. 93,13 with n. 1 (on p. 154); *in Parm.* VI 1080,12-32; VII 1157,29; *in Tim.* I 161,17; *in Alc.* 247,9.

37. In the mythological tradition fate is often represented as a spindle (or as a woman with a spindle) allotting to each soul the thread of its life span (as in the myth of Er at the end of Plato's *Republic*). *Klôthô* or 'spinster' is one of the three *moirai*. She spins the thread of life. The (rare) term *klôstêr* stands for 'spindle' or for the 'thread of fate'. It is synonymous with *nêma*. In his commentary on the myth of Er, Proclus interprets the spindle and the role of the *moirai* in an astrological sense. In his view, Plato describes the connected influence of the celestial bodies at the moment of incarnation of a particular soul, which has a 'fatal' influence on many events in one's future life. 'The ancients compared the interconnected and interwoven efficient causality resulting from all the celestial bodies with the revolution [of the spindle] together with the tension of the thread from above to below' (*in Remp.* II 343,7-10). He also refers to 'the Chaldeans and Egyptians' who can make prognostics about our future life (presumably through 'horoscopes'), see *in Remp.* II 343,4-5 and 318,12ff. The 'experts in divine matters' mentioned here are probably those Chaldean astrologers.

38. cf. *Elem. Theol.* §7, p. 8,1-2: 'Every productive cause is superior to that which it produces'. As Dodds writes in his commentary (on p. 193): 'This is the principle on which the whole structure of Neoplatonism is founded'.

39. The Platonic expression *theia moira* is often used by Neoplatonists.

40. The best commentary on this chapter is, once again, to be found in *Elem. Theol.* §§52-5 (on time and eternity) with the commentary by Dodds ad loc.

41. Plato uses the expression 'what is not, but always comes to be' in *Timaeus* (27D6-28A1) to indicate the world of becoming as distinct from the eternal intelligible being. Beings that exist in time either exist for a limited period of time (as is the case with mortal animals) or for an infinite period of time (as the celestial bodies and the world as a whole). Cf. *Elem. Theol.* §55, p. 52,15-16: 'Of things which exist in time, some have a perpetual duration, whilst others have a dated existence in a part of time.'

42. On the necessity of intermediaries, see *Elem. Theol.* §106 and Dodds' commentary ad loc. See also below, n. 95.

43. S*ympatheia* is an important element in the Stoic doctrine of fate (cf. *SVF* 2.475, 532, 534, 546). The doctrine also became an integral part of the Neoplatonic understanding of the cosmos, see Plotinus III 1 [3] 5,8 and IV 5 [29] 2-3.

44. The souls, which are incorporeal, have activities in time, though not in space.

Notes to pages 46-47

45. On *prostatis* see n. 48 and n. 257.

46. On the maintaining cause, see Steel (2003).

47. The metaphor comes from a celebrated passage in *Phaedo* (87E1-2), where Plato compares the soul to a weaver: it always weaves anew that which wears out (in the body). Cf. Proclus, *in Tim.* III 287,12 and *in Remp.* II 8,21. See also Philoponus, *Aet.* 235,28 and 236,25, who uses the image to demonstrate that the world cannot be eternal.

48. The threefold division of the soul into vegetative, sensitive, and rational is Aristotelian, but adopted by Platonists, see Proclus, *in Tim.* I 148,8-9: when the soul is incarnated, 'it first lives a vegetative life, presiding (*prostatis*) over nourishment and growth of the body'. Proclus uses the same term *prostatis* in our text to characterise nature or the vegetative power, see chs 10,19 and 12,2.

49. 'Offsprings (*ekgona*) of nature', cf. *in Tim.* I 429,6-7.

50. cf. Aristotle, *Phys.* 5.6, 230a31-b1: 'some forms of coming to be are violent and not allotted (*heimarmenai*) – contrary are those happening according to nature.' Aristotle distinguishes in this text changes contrary to nature from changes according to nature and considers the latter as *heimarmenai*. Although he does not use the phrase *par' heimarmenên*, one can deduce from what he says that he considers unusual and violent changes not only as *para phusin*, but also as *par' heimarmenên*. Cf. Simplicius, *in Phys.* 911,9-11: 'the commentators deduce from this passage that the Peripatetics put *heimarmenê* in what happens according to nature, since he called 'not *heimarmenas*' the changes that are violent and go against nature.' The 'commentators' probably refers to Alexander of Aphrodisias, see *De Fato* 6, p. 170,7-9 and *De Anima mantissa*, 180,3-26; 186,5-24. Proclus defends the same interpretation in *in Tim.* III 272,11ff.: 'Aristotle calls somewhere growth against the order, against fate (*par' heimarmenên*)'. See also Festugière (1966-8), vol. 5, pp. 148-9.

51. *Polit.* 272E5-6. On Proclus' interpretation of this cosmological myth, see *in Remp.* II 357,28-359,8. In this section, Proclus defends the same view as in his commentary. The fate governing the physical world is not a god nor an intellect nor a soul, but the nature of the universe. On the identification of nature and fate, see also *in Tim.* III 273,4ff. Proclus adopted the idea from Iamblichus (see Iamblichus [Stobaeus, *Anth.* I 81,8ff. and 81,14ff.]). See also the Introduction, p. 10.

52. *Or. Chald.* fr. 102, also quoted by Proclus, in ch. 21,3 and in *Theol. Plat.* V 32, p. 119,9-12 ('the source of nature is called by the gods the first *heimarmenê*'). See also *in Tim.* III 271,16-17. 'In the context of the theurgic rites, 'gazing' at 'nature/destiny' (or Hecate) is to invite the danger of demonic attack' (Majercik (1989), 180).

53. For an explanation of this definition of fate as nature, see the digression on nature in the prologue of the commentary on the *Timaeus* (*in Tim.* I 9,25-14,3, and in particular 12,26ff.). Cf. also Iamblichus, *Epist. ad Sop.* (Stobaeus, *Anth.* I 5,18): 'the whole essence of fate consists in nature'. For Proclus, however, fate is not simply (*haplôs*) identical with nature: see his discussion with Porphyry in *in Tim.* III 272,2-273,20. On fate and nature see also *Theol. Plat.* V 32, p. 118,24-119,26.

54. The expression *sunkukleitai* stems from *Polit.* 269C4-5, where it is said that god assists the world in its movement and 'guides it by imparting its rotation to it' (cf. also Proclus, *Theol. Plat.* V 19, p. 71,15). In this passage, however, Proclus refers to the rotation of the heavens which takes in its whirl also the sublunary bodies, and first of all the air that is adjacent to it. On this see Philoponus, *Aet.* 241,4ff. and *in Meteor.* 31,28-33.

55. For the sympathy between the celestial and the mortal things in the universe, see *in Tim.* I 412,18ff. On *sympatheia*, see also above, n. 43.

56. On time as a circularly moving image of eternity, see *Tim.* 37D. On the cyclical process in the sublunary world as imitation of the cyclical movement of the celestial spheres, see Aristotle, *Phys.* 4.14, 223b28-9: 'one says that human affairs are cyclical, and also the generation and corruption of the other things that have a natural motion'; cf. Aristotle, *GC* 2.4, 331b2-11; 2.10, 337a4-6.

57. Proclus now examines what providence is, starting from its 'common notion' which he had called in ch. 8,14 a 'source of goods'.

58. Plato, *Resp.* 2, 379C5-6.

59. *Tim.* 48A1-2. The identification of 'intellect' with 'providence' and 'necessity' with 'fate' goes back to Middle Platonism, see Numenius quoted by Calcidius, *in Tim.* 269 and 296. Proclus, however, corrects this view: the demiurge only exercises providence, insofar as he is a 'god'.

60. cf. *Polit.* 272E6 (with Proclus, *in Remp.* II 206,21-4) and *Tim.* 89C5.

61. cf. *Elem. Theol.* §80, p. 74,27-8: 'The proper nature of all bodies is to be acted upon, and of all incorporeal beings to be agents, the former being in themselves inactive and the latter impassible' (trans. Dodds, see also his commentary ad loc.).

62. Bodies act without *proairesis*, see *in Remp.* I 206,16ff.; Plotinus IV 4 [28] 13,7-12; V 4 [7] 1,28-34. On choice (*proairesis*) see below, nn. 201, 262, and the Introduction, p. 23.

63. See *Tim.* 62C-63B.

64. *Enallax* is a mathematical expression for alternation in a geometrical analogy (several occurrences can be found in Proclus' *in Eucl.*). If Providence stands to the Intelligible (P/I) as Fate to the Sensible (F/S), then one can say, *permutando*, that Providence/Fate is as Intelligible/Sensible. See Proclus, *in Tim.* I 345,3ff. and III 13,8ff.

65. See Aristotle, *DA* 1.1, 403a10-12. In his commentary on the *Enneads*, Proclus made the same observation about Aristotle's doctrine: 'Aristotle made the soul twofold, one separated from the body, one having its being in the body' (cf. Westerink, (1959), 1ff.).

66. On heart and liver as 'seats' of the irascible and the desirous part respectively, see *Tim.* 70A. See, moreover, the discussion on this in the Hellenistic tradition, summarized by Tieleman (1996), 38-60. See, finally, Steel (2001).

67. Plotinus I 1 [53] 12-13. In his commentary on this text, Proclus argues that affections are not perceptions, but always connected with perceptions; see Westerink (1959), 6.

68. Starting from below, this is already the 'third' life of the soul. In fact, however, it is the first life of the soul, since it uses the two inferior forms of life (vegetative and sensitive) which are usually called 'secondary lives'. See *in Parm.* I 663,8-9; I 678,23; III 819,25; *in Tim.* I 11,5.

69. The use of the metaphor of *epokhoumenê* ('riding upon') to describe the hierarchical relation between a superior and inferior principle is very common in Proclus. Already Plotinus uses it ten times. The first to have used it was probably Numenius.

70. For a standard example of optical illusion, see Aristotle, *DA* 3.3, 428b3. Only the Epicureans defended the view that the sun was not much larger than it appeared to be. The same example is discussed by Proclus in *in Tim.* I 249,30-250,24: to correct the illusions of sense perception we need the judgement of *doxa*.

71. See Homer, *Od.* 20.17: 'Ulysses smote his breast and chided thus his heart: Endure, my heart, for worse has thou endured.' The text is quoted by Plato, *Resp.* 3, 390D4-5 and 4, 441B6 as an example for the (Platonic) view that reason can educate the spirited element of the soul. The same quotation is used in a similar context by Plato in *Phaedo* 91D8 and 94E1. See, finally, Proclus, *in Remp.* I 155,12; 224,4.

72. The metaphor of *skirtôsa* goes back to the myth of the chariot of the soul in *Phaedr.* 254A: 'whereas the obedient horse is constrained by temperance, the other heeding no more the driver's goad or whip, springs up and dashes on.'

73. cf. *Phaedo* 81B: 'because the soul has always been associated with the body and cared for it and loved it, and has been so *beguiled* (*goêteuomenê*) by the body and its passions and pleasures [...].'

74. The image of *skiagraphia* goes back to Plato's *Phil.* 40A-C. As Socrates declares there, we are capable of painting within ourselves representations of pleasures: 'bad persons delight for the most part in false pleasures, good in true ones'.

75. See *Phaedo* 65B3-4.

76. See *Phaedo* 65D: 'have you ever seen any of these things (beauty and goodness) with your eyes?'.

77. The word *thorubos* ('confused noise of a crowded assembly') is used by Plato as a metaphor for the rumour coming from the inferior faculties of the soul, due to its incarnation. See *Tim.* 43B6; 70E7; *Phaedo* 66D6; Plotinus IV 4 [28] 17,23-6; VI 4 [22] 15,20-34; Proclus, *in Alc.* 186,14-16; *in Tim.* III 329,13ff.

78. According to *Tim.* 35B2-7 the demiurge gave the soul a harmonic composition; see Proclus' commentary ad loc. (*in Tim.* II 167,24-174,10).

79. The soul discovers itself as a *logikos kosmos*. This seems to be a correction of the provocative claim of Plotinus that 'each of us is an intelligible world' (*kosmos noêtos*) (Plotinus III 4 [15] 3,22). According to Proclus, we are not an 'intelligible world', but a 'rational world', having within our souls the *logoi* which are images of the Forms. The soul is both image and paradigm, see Steel (1993).

80. *Exethôre* is a Homeric term, used by Plotinus in a similar context; see Plotinus VI 4 [22] 16,28-30: 'the soul, which belongs to the whole intelligible universe and hides its part in the whole, leapt out, we might say, from the whole to a part'. The verb *exethôrô* is also used in the Chaldean Oracles.

81. This is again a reference to Theodore's profession as an engineer. See the Introduction, pp. 3-4.

82. For the rite of ablutions in the initiation to the mysteries, see Plato, *Crat.* 405A and Proclus, *in Crat.* 176, p. 101,3-5; *in Alc.* 9,1-7. Proclus practises himself the rites of ablutions, see Marinus, *Vita Procli* §18,27-8 and n. 5 of Saffrey-Segonds (2001) on p. 127.

83. On the role of geometry and arithmetic as propedeutic sciences in the education of the philosopher, cf. Plato, *Resp.* 7, 521C-531C.

84. The metaphor of the vantage-point (*periôpê*) comes from Plato, *Polit.* 275E5 and is very frequent in Proclus: cf. *in Alc.* 21,2; *Theol. Plat.* I 3, p. 16,1; see also below, ch. 19,16.

85. Already Plato talks about 'sister souls', but in another sense (see *Phaedo* 108B6). Proclus means here the divine souls of planets and stars, which are our sister souls, because made by the same father from the same soul-stuff, see *in Tim.* III 384,24ff. Already Plotinus II 9 [33] 18,16 and IV 3 [27] 6,13.

86. See above, n. 84.

87. For the metaphorical use of *anabakkheuô* see Plato, *Phaedr.* 234D5; 245A3; Plotinus I 6 [1] 5,4; VI 7 [38] 22,9. According to Marinus, *Vita Procli* §22,4-15, Proclus himself had this Bacchic ecstatic experience regarding the first principles: 'he was given a direct vision of the most blessed spectacle there and acquired knowledge of them, no longer reasoning in a discursive and demon-

strative way, but contemplating as it were by sight, by means of the simple intuitions of his intellectual activity, the paradigms in the divine intellect'.

88. The expression *ekgonoi theôn* comes from *Tim.* 40D: 'to know and tell the origin of the other divinities is beyond us, and we must accept the traditions of men of old time who affirm themselves to be the offspring of the gods – that is what they say – and they must surely know their ancestors'. This ironic comment on the mythological gods is taken seriously by Proclus; see his commentary ad loc. in *in Tim.* III 159,23ff. (where there is also the reference to the Sybil).

89. Famous expression from *Phaedr.* 244D3-4 (cf. also 244A4-8); cf. Hermias, *in Phaedr.* 83,15ff.; Proclus, *in Remp.* I 84,16-17; 178,24-5; *in Alc.* 48,24; *Theol. Plat.* I 4, p. 18,1.

90. The Sibyl is mentioned in Plato, *Phaedr.* 244Bff. (with commentary ad loc. of Hermias, *in Phaedr.* 94,18ff.). See Proclus, *in Tim.* III 160,1-8: 'For these souls manifest themselves from which class of gods they descend. Thus the Sibyl who oracles immediately after her birth [...] Those souls turn towards their forefathers and are filled by them with divine knowledge; their cognition is enthusiastic, since it is united to the god through divine light'. See also *in Tim.* III 282,2-6 where the Sybil is said to have declared her divine rank after her birth: 'I am intermediary between gods and human beings'.

91. The rare term *theomoiros* is also used by Damascius (*Vita Isidori* 191,1) in a story about a woman capable of foretelling future events.

92. This is the reversal of the right order proposed in *Laws*, where it is said that the sober people have to take command over the non-sober: see *Leg.* 1, 640D4ff.; 2, 671D6-7; 672A3.

93. The distinction 'according to substance' and 'according to relation (*kata skhesin*)' (cf. below, n. 202) is also used in other contexts. Thus, Proclus admits that there exist, besides the demons that are demons by nature, also souls that are demons '*qua* disposition or relation'. See *De Mal.* ch. 17 and n. 103 in Opsomer-Steel (2003), 112 (with other references). Theodore of Asine is said to have made this distinction first. He also applied it to the problem of the reincarnation of human souls in irrational animal bodies. See Steel (2005), 182.

94. The expression comes from *Tim.* 41E2-3. On the interpretation of this passage see Proclus, *in Tim.* III 277,5ff.

95. See *Elem. Theol.* §28, which formulates the principle of continuity governing the procession of all things. As Dodds writes in his commentary (quoting precisely this passage from our treatise): 'As there is no void in the physical universe, so there is none in the spiritual [...] There are no gaps in the divine devolution' (p. 216). To preserve the continuity in the procession of all things, intermediary terms have to be introduced diminishing the dissimilarity between the extremes. Already Aristotle said that nature does not jump: between the different classes of animals there are always intermediaries filling the gaps (see *HA* 9.1, 588b4-10). Plotinus is the first to have made this a general ontological principle explaining the procession of all things from the First. Proclus gives an excellent formulation of the principle in *Theol. Plat.* III 2, p. 6,21-4: 'If the procession of all beings has to be continuous and no void comes between them, neither among incorporeal beings nor among bodies, what comes forth in each nature must proceed through similitude'. For the influence of this principle in the history of ideas, see Lovejoy (1936).

96. The 'divinis illis' is probably a reference to the theurgists who received the revelation of the oracles. Cf. *in Alc.* 53,1.

97. cf. *Or. Chald.* fr. 102 and notes; the same text is quoted by Proclus, *Theol. Plat.* V 32, p. 119,12 and *in Tim.* III 271,16-17. In both texts Proclus also makes a connection with *Tim.* 41E2-3 (quoted above in n. 94).

98. See *Or. Chald.* fr. 103, which is only attested here and in Psellus, see *Philosophica Minora*, vol. 2, p. 143,19 ed. Duffy-O'Meara (without the last words 'cuius finis'). The Latin manuscripts all have a lacuna after 'finis': whereas Kroll added [*ouden*], Lewy (1956), 266, n. 23, instead conjectures *Haidês* as the missing noun.

99. See *Or. Chald.* fr. 153: 'for the theurgists do not fall into the herd which is subject to fate' and fr. 154 'who are going in herds'. The 'herds' stand for the masses of human beings who live a life dominated by the passions. Cf. Iamblichus, *De Myst.* 5.18 and Proclus, *in Alc.* 245,6-8.

100. See *Or. Chald.* fr. 130 and Proclus, *in Tim.* III 266,18-23. I agree with Lewy (1956), 212, n. 142, who suggests that the introductory formula 'understanding the works of the father' (which is also a part of fr. 40) may have made up the first verse of the Oracle. Cf. Majercik (1989), 190 ad loc. See also the Philological Appendix.

101. As Strobel noticed, this is a reference to *Phaedo* 82D3 (reading *sômata*, not *sômati*).

102. See Plotinus III 4 [15] 6,47-56: 'the soul embarks first of all in this universe as if in a boat, then the nature which has the name of the 'spindle' takes it over and sets it, just as in a ship, in some seat of fortune. And as the circuit of heaven, like a wind, carries round the man sitting, or even moving about, on the ship [...] he is moved either by the tossing of the ship or by himself of his own impulse'. The same metaphor is developed in *in Remp.* II 345,14ff. Proclus also took inspiration from the celebrated text in *Resp.* 6, 488Bff. where the philosopher risks being brutalised by the sailors.

103. According to Westerink (1962), 162, Proclus is 'referring in this passage to a personal experience, which had already been mentioned by Theodore'. It may have been an anti-pagan attack in Athens (leading to the destruction of his house?) which caused Proclus' precipitate flight to Asia. See Marinus, *Vita Procli* §15,14-35 and my Introduction, pp. 1-2. See also Saffrey (1992).

104. cf. Plotinus I 4 [46] 7,23ff.: 'If he thought that the ruin of his city were a great evil [...] there would be no virtue left in him if he thought that woods and stones, and the death of mortals, were important'.

105. *Aretê adespotos* is a celebrated Platonic axiom (*Resp.* 10, 617E3), quoted by all later philosophical schools. In his treatise on the myth of Er, Proclus devotes an interesting discussion to the interpretation of the expression *a-despotos*, 'without master' (*in Remp.* II 275,19-277,7). Amelius asked what exactly then is so special about virtue that it is characterised as *adespoton*. Is not vice also *adespoton*, since both virtue and vice depend on us? Proclus replies that virtue is called *adespoton*, not only because it depends on us, but also because it liberates us from servitude to passions and the external goods and makes us free and masters, whereas vice, though depending on us, makes us slaves.

106. The 'money loving' part is just another name for the desirous part of the soul, see *Resp.* 9, 580E.

107. The region around the heart refers to the seat of the desirous part of the soul. Cf. above, n. 66.

108. In its descent to the body the soul takes on more and more 'garments' (from the celestial spheres and the elements through which it passes) until it is imprisoned in the fat earthly body; in its ascent, the soul takes off one by one those additional clothes and returns 'naked' to its origin; see *Elem. Theol.* §209 with the notes of Dodds' commentary ad loc. on pp. 306-9; *De Mal.* 24,29ff. with n. 176 of Opsomer-Steel (2003), 116; *in Tim.* I 112,19-113,11; III 297,20-281,2; *in Alc.* 138,15-22 (bibliographical references by Segonds in n. 5 on p. 203); *in Alc.* 179,15-18; 257,3-5.

109. Self-determination in the strict sense is only found among the gods, see below, chs 56-61.

110. For the first expression see n. 105; the second (much less quoted!) phrase comes from Plato's *Alc.* 135C6-10.

111. That vice is not really a power, but an infirmity, is Socrates' argument in *Resp.* 4, 444D-E. See also Proclus, *De Mal.* 52-3 and Steel (1998), 99-101.

112. For the distinction between the instrument and the user of the instrument, see *in Remp.* I 171,22-172,6 where Proclus refers to *Alc.* 129Bff. See also *in Remp.* II 260,5ff.

113. The term *ethelodouleia* refers to *Symp.* 184C6 where Socrates talks about the willing and complete subjection of the lover to his beloved. Proclus is the first to have used this term for the free servitude of the virtuous soul. That moral freedom consists in obeying god, is also a common Stoic doctrine, see Seneca: 'In regno nati sumus: deo parere libertas nostra' (*De Vita Beata*, 15.7). In the Stoic view, however, the god we have to obey is fate identical with providence.

114. The souls 'govern the whole world' if they follow Zeus and the other gods 'ordering all things and taking care of them' (*Phaedr.* 246E4-6). Cf. below, ch. 60 and *in Alc.* 149,1-8.

115. *Phaedr.* 246C1-2.

116. It is a privilege of the gods to exercise authority over all things. When the souls lead a divine life, they become as gods and govern with them the whole world: see below, ch. 60 and n. 269. But the souls who are dominated by the irrational forces, become slaves of fate. See n. 119.

117. As Erler observes, this is a reference to the famous dictum of Archimedes, fr. 15,2 Heiberg. See also the Introduction, p. 3.

118. Proclus probably means that criminals, when undergoing punishment, had to put on masks with 'a smile' as if they were enjoying their torture. There is no confirmation in other sources of this 'Egyptian' practice.

119. cf. *in Tim.* III 277,18-20: 'when the souls are dominated by the mortal kind of soul, they become slaves of fate: for the universe uses them as irrational beings'.

120. On evil as infirmity, see n. 111.

121. As Strobel informed me, this is an implicit quotation from Plotinus, I 1 [53] 2,12-14. According to Plotinus the soul is never cut off from the intelligible world; see IV 8 [6] 8,1-13. See Sorabji (2004a), 3(e). The quotation is surprising, because Proclus elsewhere criticises Plotinus' view, see Steel (1978), 46-7. See also below, n. 232.

122. On this third problem and the distinction between the different forms of knowledge, see the Introduction, pp. 16-17.

123. It is Proclus' intention 'to say what we consider to be in accordance with reality and with the most illustrious of former philosophers' (ch. 1). This is Proclus' goal in all his commentaries, cf. *in Eucl.* 50,16-18: 'arguments in accordance with the reality itself and with the teaching of Plato'; *in Remp.* II 96,8; *in Alc.* 92,2; *in Tim.* III 235,11; 266,1.

124. That *doxa* only knows the individual fact (*oti*) and not the universal nor the cause (*dioti*), is often said by Proclus, see *in Tim.* I 248,10ff.; *in Remp.* I 263,30-264,3.

125. On the importance of *doxa* for practical life, see *Meno* 97B where it is said that true opinion is sufficient for the right praxis. In *Theaet.* 187A5-6, the name *doxa* is given to the disposition of the soul, who has left sense perception and 'is occupied with beings by itself'.

126. Diogenes Laertius (5.31) uses *metriopatheia* for the Aristotelian ethical idea, opposing it to Stoic *apatheia*. For the Neoplatonic philosophers, however, there is no opposition, but subordination. See Porphyry, *Sent*. 32,29-35: 'The disposition characteristic of the civic virtues is to be seen as the imposition of measure on the passions (*metriopatheia*) since it has as its aim living a human life in accordance with nature, while the disposition that results from the contemplative virtues is manifested in total detachment from the passions (*apatheia*), which has as its aim assimilation to God' (trans. Dillon (2005)). As Porphyry, Proclus emphasises the role of the virtues in the process of purification. On the transformation of *katharsis*, see also Lautner (2000).

127. For the expression 'scenery of passions' see *in Remp*. I 124,13.

128. The proverbial phrase comes from *Gorg*. 493D5-6 (see also below, n. 287). What follows is a remarkable synthesis of the Platonic and Aristotelian theory of knowledge, see the Introduction, pp. 16-17.

129. Summary of the argument in *Resp*. 6, 510B-511D. See also below, ch. 50.

130. That is dialectic, on which further in ch. 29.

131. Aristotle, *Phys*. 1.2, 185a1; cf. *Metaph*. 11.6, 1063b10; *An. Post*. 1.12, 77b3ff.

132. Use of a Platonic phrase, cf. *Phil*. 26D7 (Strobel).

133. Proclus describes here the method of dialectic, combining *Resp*. 6, 511B6, 534C1 ('through all forms towards the unconditional') and *Phaedr*. 265D-266B on the procedures of division and synopsis: 'making the one multiple' and 'the multiple one' (the formulation itself is inspired by *Tim*. 68D4-7; *Parm*. 157A4-6; cf. *in Parm*. I 656,2-5; *in Remp*. II 225,14ff.).

134. *Resp*. 7, 534E2-3; *Epinomis* 992A1. The same texts are quoted in *in Eucl*. 42,9ff. where the different interpretations of the metaphors are analysed. See also below, n. 234.

135. cf. Aristotle, *Metaph*. 13.8, 1084b23ff.; see also below, ch. 50.

136. On these four procedures of dialectic, see *in Parm*. V 980,17-982,30.

137. The term *epibolê* is used for simple intuition, grasp, perception, to be distinguished from insight through reasoning; the term *autoptic* belongs to the religious vocabulary of revelations: 'a vision without mediation, face to face'.

138. See Aristotle, *An. Post*. 1.2, 72b24. This passage is often quoted by the Neoplatonist commentators as an argument that Aristotle too accepted the doctrine of the Forms: cf. Ps.-Simplicius, *in DA* 124,23; Philoponus, *in DA* 3,27; 543,2. See also Proclus, *in Tim*. I 438,29-30 and *in Alc*. 247,2-4 and n. 6 of Segonds (on pp. 419-20).

139. See *Tim*. 37C1-3 and Proclus, *in Tim*. II 312,9ff.

140. See Plotinus I 2 [19] 8,13; I 1 [53] 9,12; see also VI 9 [9] 8,27 and VI 7[38] 35,21.

141. Platonic phrase, e.g. in *Phaedr*. 252A5 (Strobel).

142. The term *thixis* is used by Proclus as a metaphor together with *epaphê* to indicate the direct grasp of the intelligible object by the intellect; cf. *Theol. Plat*. IV 12, p. 41,26-42,2: 'contact (*epaphê*) is found on many levels, even in incorporeal beings, in the sense of a communion of the first with the inferior, and philosophers are accustomed to call these communions contacts (*sunaphas*) and the touching (*thixeis*) of thought *epaphas*' (see Saffrey-Westerink, with complementary notes 1 and 2 on pp. 145-6); cf. also *in Parm*. III 809,6. The same terminology is also found in Hermias, *in Phaedr*. 19,24-6; 64,16-17: 'as it were by touch and contact of the intellect'.

143. *Edaisato* is a poetical term. If this is a first part of a hexameter, it could be an otherwise unknown fragment from the Chaldean Oracles.

144. On madness beyond intellect, see above, n. 89.

145. One may find a beautiful parallel in the *Commentary on the Parmenides*: 'How else are we to become nearer to the One, if we do not rouse up the One of the soul? [...] Rousing up the one within us we may connect ourselves

Notes to pages 56-58

to the One itself' (*in Parm.* VI 1071,26; 1072,8; cf. 1081,4). See also *in Alc.* 247,8-14. Iamblichus is said to have been the first to develop this doctrine of the 'one in us', as one may conclude from his interpretation of the myth of the winged chariot: see Hermias, *in Phaedr.* 150,24ff. (= fr. 6 Dillon). It is Iamblichus again who identified this 'one' with the 'flower of the intellect' of the Chaldean Oracles (see *Or. Chald.* fr. 1,1).

146. On this principle (that goes back to Presocratic philosophy, see Aristotle, *DA* 1.2, 405b15), see *Theol. Plat.* I 3, p. 15,17-18 and n. 3 (on pp. 135-6); *in Alc.* 247,14 and n. 9 (where other parallel texts are quoted).

147. The term *hupernoousa* is quite rare, cf. Plotinus VI 8 [39] 16,32 (*hupernoêsis*).

148. On the mystical silence, required at the revelation of the gods, see Majercik (1989), 148, note to fragment 16, Beierwaltes (1972), 364-6.

149. See Plotinus VI 9 [9] 10,11-12: 'when he sees, he will see himself as like this, or rather he will be in union with himself as like this (...) since he has become single and simple. But perhaps one should not say: will see'.

150. cf. *Or. Chald.* fr. 1,1 (with note of Majercik (1989), 138); cf. above, n. 146.

151. On the rest and peace of the soul, see *Theol. Plat.* II 11, p. 44,1-22 (with notes of Saffrey-Westerink).

152. The term *diarthrôsis* (articulation) is of Stoic origin, cf. the title of Chrysippus' work: 'articulation of our (logical) ethical concepts' (*SVF* 2.13; 2.16).

153. The celestial Moirai, daughters of necessity, are introduced in the myth of Er (*Resp.* 10, 617B8-D2). See Proclus' long commentary in *in Remp.* II 339,19-253,17.

154. On this argument and its refutation, see the Introduction, pp. 17-19.

155. On self-love (*philautia*), see Plato, *Leg.* 5, 731Eff.; Aristotle, *EN* 9.8, 1168a30-1169b1.

156. The phrase 'nothing episodic' comes from Aristotle, cf. *Metaph.* 14.3, 1090b19 ('nature is not episodic as a bad tragedy'). It is often quoted to stress the ordered structure of the world which cannot be ruined by luck and fortune. See Iamblichus, *Ep. ad Maced.* (Stobaeus, *Anth.* II 175,1 W.-H.). For Proclus, see *De Mal.* 50,36 and n. 353 of Opsomer-Steel (2003), 127.

157. On the notion of *kairos* and its role in divine providence, see Proclus, *in Alc.* 120,12-124,27 (on *kairos* in the encounter of Socrates and Alcibiades) with the notes of Segonds (1985); see also *in Remp.* II 79,19-24. On this passage, see also Brunner (1992) and (1997) and O'Meara (2003).

158. *Leg.* 4, 709B7-C3, which is also quoted in the discussion on *kairos* in *in Alc.* 124,12-13.

159. For *kairos heimarmenos*, cf. *in Alc.* 124,11 and the Philological Appendix.

160. The three causes of what happens are: (1) god; (2) fortune (*kairos*); and (3) our own skill.

161. On human life as a part in a universal drama, see above, n. 6 and the Introduction, p. 13.

162. The image of the dance of the souls comes from the myth of *Phaedr.* 250B. The souls when following Zeus and the other Olympic gods behold 'amidst that happy chorus (*khorô*)' beauty in all its brightness and enjoy all the other blessed visions. There is a famous adaptation of the metaphor in Plotinus VI 9 [9] 8,37-45: 'we truly dance our god-inspired dance around him'.

163. See Plato, *Leg.* 10, 904B: 'the demiurge has given the different places and regions such a qualification that they may receive the appropriate types of souls, but he left the cause of the formation of a particular quality (*poion ti*) [of life] to our individual choices.' For an interpretation of this text, see Proclus, *in Remp.* II 358,1-359,6.

164. The reference to the celebrated Delphic maxim 'know yourself' shows that the 'oracles' here must not be understood exclusively as the *Chaldean Oracles*. On the interpretation of this section, see Westerink (1962), 163-4. On the Delphic maxim and its importance in Neoplatonic philosophy, see *in Alc.* 5,3-14 (with n. 4 of Segonds (1985), 128); cf. Steel (2006). The first oracle is also quoted in the same context in *in Alc.* 129,24-5 (Segonds (1985), 107, n. 5). To explain the meaning of the exhortation to put on clothes, we may refer to the Pauline exhortation in *Ephes.* 4.24: 'invest you with the new man'.

165. cf. *Tim* 88A on the diseases of the body caused by the soul.

166. That choice is not absolute freedom will be discussed below (chs 56-61, problem 7). Hierocles defended the same view in his treatise *On Providence*: 'our self-determination (*autexousion*) is not of the sort that it can change everything that is and comes to be through its own voluntary movements [...] Hence it is reasonable that the power of human self-determination, being mobile and ephemeral, is completely impotent in regard to the creation or alteration of anything if there is no co-operation from outside. Human choice has power over nothing but itself, of making itself better or worse by its dispositions' (cod. 251, 465a40ff.; trans. Schibli, 356-7, modified).

167. A similar argument is to be found in *in Remp.* II 259,23ff.

168. On this argument and its refutation, see the Introduction, p. 18.

169. Though *philomanteutai* is very rare, it occurs already in Plato, cf. *Leg.* 7, 813D4.

170. *Motus* must refer here (as further in l. 17 'circulatione') to the celestial movements and their influence on sublunary events, cf. *in Remp.* II 274,6.

171. That 'nature does nothing in vain' is a celebrated Aristotelian principle. See e.g. Aristotle, *Cael.* 1.4, 271a33; 1.11, 291b13; *DA* 3.9, 432b21; 3.12, 434a31; *Pol.* 1.2, 1253a9; 1.8, 1256b21. It is often used by Proclus, see *in Alc.* 162,16; 238,16 (see Segonds (1986), 226, n. 2); *in Parm.* III 791,24; *in Tim.* II 90,30.

172. In which sense prayers can still be useful if everything is determined by fate? This question is quite often raised in the philosophical debate on determinism, see Alexander, *De Fato* 17; [Plut.], *De Fato* 574E; Nemesius, *De Nat. Hom.* 295-306, p. 106,29ff.; Iamblichus, *De Myst.* 5.26; Proclus, *in Tim.* I 207,21-214,12; Boethius, 5, pr. 3, 33-4.

173. As Westerink (1962), 164, noticed, this is a reference to *Resp.* 3, 398A. Socrates speaks about an exceptional poet having the capacity 'of imitating all things'. 'Should he arrive in our city, we should fall down and worship him as a holy and wondrous and delightful creature'; alas, we should also tell him that here is no place for someone of his kind in our city: 'we should send him away to another city, after pouring myrrh down over his head and crowning him with fillets of wool'. It is surprising that Proclus uses this ironical comment on the banishment of the poets from the city to talk about the banishment of the priests.

174. *Rheumata* (literally 'streams') is a term used in Chaldean context for the influences coming from the celestial bodies, cf. Lewy (1956), 266; 291 n. 126.

175. cf. *Tim.* 27C1-3, which is the classic text in all debates on the necessity of prayer.

176. This may refer to the famous oracle of Apollo to Laius, often debated in the discussion on the utility of oracles, see Alexander, *De Fato*, 31, p. 202,8ff., with commentary in Sharples (1983).

177. The distinction between two types of divination is traditional (already in Homer, *Od.* 20.100ff.) and was developed by the Stoics (see Cicero, *De Divinatione* 1.11). Iamblichus devotes a long discussion to this distinction in *De Myst.* 3.27.

178. On the possible effect of theurgical practices to remove diseases, see Psellus, *Philosophica Minora*, I, opusc. 3, 150-5, p. 9. ed. O'Meara.

179. The image of the balance comes from Plato, *Resp.* 8, 550E7.

180. On this problem, see the Introduction, pp. 18-19.

181. Literally 'the ways according to education'. This expression is taken from *Tim.* 53C2, where it refers to the mathematical sciences. See Proclus, *in Eucl.* 20,10; *Theol. Plat.* I 2, p. 11,5 and Simplicius, *in Cael.* 641,26.

182. cf. *Phaedr.* 250B2.

183. cf. above, ch. 16,3ff. (though there is no discussion there on self-reflection). On self-reflection, see *Elem. Theol.* §15, p. 16,30 ('All that is capable of reverting upon itself is incorporeal'); *Elem. Theol.* §16 p. 18,7-8 ('All that is capable of reverting upon itself has an existence separable from all body'); §§82-3. See also *in Tim.* II 286,32ff. See also Steel (2006).

184. On the soul being buried in the body, see Plato, *Crat.* 400C; *Gorg.* 492E.

185. cf. *Leg.* 10, 892B1.

186. On the relation between soul and ether, see the Introduction, p. 19.

187. *Tim.* 41D4-5. On the interpretation of the figure of the 'crater' in the Neoplatonic tradition, see Proclus, *in Tim.* III 246,29-250,28.

188. The metaphor of the crater is used in *Or. Chald.* fr. 42,3. The empyrean is the highest sphere of heavens above the ethereal realm (of stars and planets) and the material sublunary world. The distinction between the three realms of the cosmos comes from the Chaldean Oracles, see Proclus, *in Tim.* II 44,29ff. and 57,10ff.; *in Remp.* II 201,2ff.; Psellus, *Or. Chald.* in *Philosophica Minora*, II, p. 146,9-12 ed. Duffy-O'Meara. For the doctrine, see Lewy (1956), 137, n. 270. On the significance of the empyrean heaven in ancient cosmology, see Maurach (1968).

189. The *zôogonos thea* is Rhea (identical with Hecate in the Chaldean tradition), the second of the intellectual gods, standing between Kronos and Zeus. See Proclus, *Theol. Plat.* V 11; *in Crat.* 143, p. 81,2-15; *in Tim.* I 5,35; 11,19-20; II 151,9; III 249,14-15.

190. Lewy (1956), 265, n. 21, gives a Greek retroversion of the end of this chapter.

191. See ch. 41.

192. On the role of the mathematical sciences in the education of the soul, see *Resp.* 7, 522C-531C.

193. See above, ch. 17,20: 'looking at its internal reasons'; see also Plotinus I 6 [1] 9,1.

194. Sense perception only grasps the 'fact'. Cf. Aristotle, *Metaph.* 1.1, 981a28-9 and *An. Post.* 1.13, 79a3ff.

195. This often repeated principle is a Neoplatonic adaptation of the Aristotelian principle of the priority of act over potency, see *in Parm.* II 754,13-15; III 823,3ff.; IV 879,39ff., *in Alc.* 88,5; *Elem. Theol.* §24.

196. The opposition between 'play' and 'serious activities' is of course Platonic. Never, however, does Plato consider sense perception as 'playful knowledge' compared to the serious business of science. On the contrary, Plato considers sometimes the sciences themselves as a sort of innocent amusement (*Tim.* 59C-D).

197. cf. *Tim.* 42A5 (66C6) where it is said that once the soul is implanted in the body, it has 'sense perception from violent affections'. Proclus explains this expression in *in Tim.* III 286,2-7: 'the corporeal life is involved in matter, which knows what comes upon it from outside and does not belong to itself, but to the body using it, and is mixed with the material masses and knows whatever it knows by undergoing an affection'.

198. The discussion on the criteria of knowledge dominates the philosophical debate in Hellenistic philosophy. In all schools we find treatises on the criteria. This discussion continued in Middle and Neo-Platonism. Proclus devotes an important digression to this question in *in Tim.* I 254,19ff. (cf. Festugière (1966-8), vol. 2, p. 93, n. 1). In his view, the *logos* is the ultimate criterion, though it may also use other criteria.

199. For the phrase *oikothen* (literally 'from inside the house'), see *in Alc.* 250,5-10: 'all this makes clear that the souls do not gather knowledge from sensible objects, but that they put forward knowledge from inside and correct what is imperfect in the phenomena'. See also above, ch. 17.

200. For *autenergêtos* see below, n. 256.

201. Choice (*proairesis*) does not belong to bodies or to forms of life involved in matter, but is characteristic of the rational soul, cf. above, n. 62 and below, n. 262. See also the Introduction, p. 23.

202. On the distinction between 'relationally' and 'essentially', cf. above, n. 93.

203. On the intermediary state of the rational soul between sense perception and intellect, see below, nn. 242 and 265; see also Plotinus V 3[49] 3,34-9 and 44-5 (quoted below at the end of ch. 59, see n. 265).

204. The opposition between what is good by 'nature' and good by 'convention' (*nomos*) is a common theme in the ethical debate in the fifth/fourth century BC. The term *thesei* ('arbitrarily') however, points to a Hellenistic source. On this presentation of hedonism, see the Introduction, p. 20.

205. This passage might be seen as an indication that Proclus wrote this treatise late in his career, when he was already an 'old man'. See the Introduction, p. 1.

206. cf. *Parm.* 130E4.

207. This is the ideal way Plato behaved. See *in Remp.* I 89,26; II 269,1. The expression 'leader intellect' comes from Plato, *Leg.* 1, 631D5 (12, 963A8); see also *Theol. Plat.* I 2, p. 11,8; V 9, p. 31,25. The maxim 'to make the intellect leader' is also attributed to Solon, see Diogenes Laertius 1.60. For the intellect corresponding to old age, see *in Parm.* I 683,23ff.

208. See Plato, *Resp.* 6, 505D and Proclus, *in Remp.* I 220,21ff.

209. For this poetical metaphor, see Plato, *Resp.* 5, 475B2-3, probably drawing from Pindar (Strobel).

210. See Aristotle, *Phys.* 1.1, 185a11; 1.3, 186a9.

211. The upward stature of human beings versus the down to earth irrational animals has become a favourite *topos* in philosophical literature since Plato's *Tim.* 90A. It also became very popular among Christian authors, see for instance Gregory of Nyssa, *De Opif. Hom.* 8.

212. This expression is taken from Plato, *Gorg.* 509A1-2 and also used in *De Decem Dub.* 1,1; *in Remp.* I 167,16.

213. cf. *Phil.* 67B1-3.

214. The *Philebus* is entirely devoted to the discussion of hedonism. In *Gorgias* 492D-506D, Socrates attacks the hedonistic position of Callicles. In *Republic* 9, 583B-588A, Socrates argues that the philosophical life is the most pleasurable one. The thesis that the good is identical with the pleasurable is criticised in *Phil.* 60A-B (cf. Damascius, *in Philebum* §214), in *Gorg.* 495A-506D and in *Resp.* 505B-D (cf. Proclus, *in Remp.* I, 272,20ff.).

215. As Westerink (1962), 164, notices, this is a quotation of a Homeric phrase, *Od.* 12.453. The same phrase is used in the same context in *in Remp.* II 309,22-3. This Homeric quotation was very popular and is to be found in Plutarch (*De Garrulitate* 504D; *Amatorius* 764A6) and other authors of the imperial period.

Notes to pages 63-64

216. cf. *Gorg.* 500D9-10; Plotinus VI 7 [38] 19,1-3: 'Shall we then hand over the decision to desire and to the soul and, trusting in the soul's experience (*pathos*), maintain that what is desired by this is good, and not enquire why it desires?'

217. As Plato argues in *Republic*, there are three different types of life according to the dominance of one of the three parts of the soul. We find those three types not only in the different life styles of individuals, but also in the different constitutions and modes of life of the states. In an important transitional passage (*Resp.* 4, 435E), Socrates argues that the forms and qualities that exist in each soul are also to be found in the states. 'It would be ridiculous to suppose that spiritedness was not derived in the states from the private citizens who are reputed to have this quality, as the populations of the Thracian and Scythian lands and generally the northern regions, or the quality of love of knowledge, which would chiefly be attributed to the region where we dwell [Greece], or the love of money which we might say is not least likely to be found in Phoenicians and the population of Egypt.' Proclus refers to those three populations in *in Remp.* I 221,20ff. (see next note). If in this text the Persians (because mentioned by Theodore) replace the Scyths (connected with the Persians in *Leg.* 1, 637D7), the 'other people' must be the Greeks.

218. See Homer, *Od.* 19.163 often quoted and already by Socrates in *Apol.* 34D. The same quotation is used by Proclus in exactly the same context in *in Remp.* I 221,12ff.

219. In *Resp.* 10, 588C-D, Socrates compares the three parts of the soul to respectively 'a many-headed beast', an animal 'with the form of lion' and one with a 'human form'. This image will become very popular among all Platonists. See also Proclus, *in Remp.* I 225,16ff.

220. See *Gorg.* 500D9-10 (Strobel).

221. See Aristotle, *EN* 7.12, 1153a15-b11. On this famous definition of pleasure in Aristotle and its interpretation by the Neoplatonist philosophers, see Van Riel (2000).

222. Already in Aristotle, it is argued that our supreme happiness lies in the activity of the better part in us. We are not identical with this rational part, since we also have a body and the psychic faculties related to it. Yet, we are 'most of all' (*malista*) this better part of us. See Aristotle, *EN* 10.7, 1177a19-20 and 1178a5-8.

223. On this problem, see the Introduction, pp. 20-2.

224. cf. *Apol.* 20E-23B and other texts quoted in the Introduction, p. 21.

225. cf. *Phaedo* 66D7-8.

226. cf. *Resp.* 7, 533D4-6.

227. cf. *Resp.* 7, 533B8-C1.

228. cf. above, chs 27-32 (the third preliminary distinction).

229. To achieve 'the supreme rank', i.e. after returning to the intelligible from the body.

230. *Phaedo* 66D7-8; 68A1.

231. The phrase *grossum hoc vinculum* refers to the fleshy body. The metaphor of the body as fetter or as bond of the soul goes back to Plato, *Phaedo* 67D1. The adjective *grossus* (*pakhus*) is often used to characterise matter and body, see *in Remp.* II 281,2 and *in Alc.* 179,17-18.

232. This is a reference (unnoticed in the scholarly literature) to a celebrated debate in the Neoplatonic school after Plotinus. Plotinus argued that the superior part of the rational soul always remains in the intelligible world, even when the soul has come down to animate the body: 'our soul has not sunk entirely, but there is always something of it in the intelligible world' (Plotinus IV 8 [6] 8,1-3). See above, n. 121. According to Plotinus, the soul always enjoys the contemplative life, and not only the inferior purificative virtues. See Plotinus I 4 [46] 9-10 and the commentary by Brittain (2002). Since Iamblichus, this doctrine was rejected by all later Neoplatonists and, hence, also by Proclus: see *Elem. Theol.* §211; *in Tim.* III 277,5; 333,29ff.; 165,7ff. On this debate see Steel (1978), 34ff. and Sorabji (2004a), 3(e). Proclus presents here a moderate solution: Though it is possible for some souls to engage in contemplation when still being in the body, such souls cannot be called 'perfectly contemplative'. For only their activity is contemplative; they do not have a full contemplative life. See also above, ch. 5.

233. *Theaet.* 173E6-174A1 (the quotation in Plato in fact comes from Pindar). The same reference in a similar context is found in *in Tim.* III 277,11-16.

234. *Resp.* 7, 534E2-3; see also above, n. 134.

235. cf. *Phaedo* 66B8ff. and also Plotinus II 9 [33] 7,2ff.

236. Since Aristotle (*EN* 1.5, 1095b14ff.), it is common to distinguish three types of life: *bios theôrêtikos, bios politikos*, and the life of pleasure. Proclus argues that a fully contemplative life here is not possible for the soul, since its activity is always interrupted. That such a life is more than human is also admitted by Aristotle, cf. Aristotle, *EN* 10.7, 1177b26-31. On the distinction between *theôria* and *theôrêtikos bios*, cf. Dudley (1999), 89-91, 107-8.

237. cf. *Resp.* 7, 533D4-6.

238. cf. *Resp.* 6, 510B7; 511B6. On Proclus' interpretation of the comparison of the divided line, see *in Remp.* I 287,20ff.

239. The author of the *Prolegomena* gives two arguments of Proclus against the authenticity of the *Epinomis*: (1) as the *Laws* are certainly the last work of Plato, it is difficult to explain how Plato himself could he have written a supplement to it; (2) in *Epinomis* planetary movement is explained in a way contrary to what one finds in the authentic dialogues; see *Prol. Plat.* 25,3-12 with the notes of Westerink-Segonds, p. 73. Cf. also *in Remp.* II 134,5ff. and *in Eucl.* 42,9ff. (in the same context). On the question of the authenticity of the *Epinomis* in Antiquity, see Tarán (1975), 115-39.

240. See above, ch. 29,6-7 and n. 134.

241. cf. *Apol.* 21A6-7. For Socrates' interpretation of the Delphic oracle, cf. *Apol.* 21Bff. On the interpretation of Socratic ignorance see also Hermias, *in Phaedr.* 31,4-9. Cf. Olympiodorus, *in Phaed.* 51,1. See also Courcelle (1974-5).

242. On the rational soul as intermediary between sense perception and intellect, see above, n. 203 and below, n. 265.

243. See *Soph.* 249C6-8.

244. On the liberation of the chains of the body, see *Phaedo* 67C and above, n. 231.

245. This is a summary of the different levels of knowledge that have already been discussed in chs 27-32.

246. On this problem, see the Introduction, p. 22.

247. The expression '*kata noun*' literally means 'according to intellect' and is often opposed to '*kata tukhên*', 'fortuituous'; see Proclus, *Theol. Plat.* II 2, p. 22,14-18.

248. See Plotinus III 2 [47] 6,1-6: 'As for people getting what they do not deserve, when the good get what is bad and the bad the opposite [...] How can this be right distribution?' Cf. Iamblichus, *Ep. ad Maced.* (Stobaeus, *Anth.* II 175,17ff. W.-H.): 'why are distributions not according to merit?'; for Theodore, see Deuse, fr. 39 (with commentary).

249. The rare term 'healed' (*exantês*) occurs first in the Hippocratic writings in the sense of 'being healed from a disease or a poison'. See also Plato, *Phaedr.* 244E2.

250. Proclus may think of the (economical) exchange of external goods, as clothes, food, etc. We only claim compensation in exchange of those goods to which we have contributed (e.g. producing corn or making clothes). When the external good just comes from a universal cause (as water coming from a source), we can ask no compensation corresponding to our merits.

251. The combination of 'persuasion' and 'force' comes from Plato; see *Resp.* 8, 554C12-D2; *Polit.* 296B1; *Leg.* 4, 711C-B. Cf. also Plotinus I 2 [19] 1,52-3: 'but we must make our argument persuasive, and not be content to force argument'. The word 'force' here stands for the polemical argument used against Theodore (*reductio in absurdum*) in the previous paragraph. In the following, a direct and convincing argument will follow.

252. See above, n. 166.

253. This is a reference to the celebrated *Enchiridion* of Epictetus (see also the Philological Appendix). It is the only passage where Epictetus is quoted directly by Proclus. Yet, the distinction between what does depend on us and what does not depend on us evidently had a profound impact on Proclus' views on human freedom. On the reception of Epictetus' *Handbook* in the Neoplatonic School, see the introduction to the edition of Simplicius' *Commentary on the Enchiridion* by I. Hadot (2001), lxxiii-c.

254. Namely Plotinus, Theodore, and Iamblichus, mentioned above; see n. 248.

255. On this question, see the Introduction, pp. 23-4.

256. Theodore characterises 'what depends on us' as *autoperigrapton* and *auto-energêton*. The latter term is not infrequent in later Neoplatonism, and in particular in Proclus, who uses it often regarding the soul. As a self-moving principle, the soul is not only acted upon, but is also always self-activating (as is clear in the process of knowledge). See above, ch. 44,16; *in Alc.* 248,15-17; 279,25-7; *in Eucl.* 15,26ff. The first term '*autoperigrapton*' is nowhere else attested. Damascius, however, uses the term *autoperigraphos* nine times, in the sense of 'what circumscribes or contains one self', and this usage is particular to him alone. In his edition, Combès translates 'ce qui se circonscrit soi-même' (cf. *in Parm.*, II, p. 100, n. 2; III, p. 23, n. 4). One may note that, in patristic and Byzantine texts, the term *aperigraptos* is often used to characterise god, who alone is infinite.

257. The expression *prôtos prostatês pantôn tôn ontôn* (*primus preses omnium entium*) to indicate god is extremely rare. I could only find a parallel in Eusebius, *Praep. Evang.* 1.1: *ton mega prostatên kai pambasilea tôn holôn*. Is Theodorus influenced here by the language of the dominant Christian religion? The term *prostatês*, however, to indicate a ruler or leader or a particular god is not uncommon. Proclus uses it, e.g., for Ares (*in Remp.* I 69,2), Hephaistos (*in Parm.* III 829,11), and the demons. Further, in chs 10,19 and 12,22 of this treatise, he calls 'fate' the *prostatês* of the corporeal realm.

258. The term *dokêsis* is of Stoic origin and first attested in Chrysippus' definition of a *phantasma* as a *dokêsis dianoias* (*SVF* 2.55). Yet, the distinction Proclus makes between a true will (*boulêsis*) and an apparent wish of what *seems* to be good (but can be bad) is not Stoic, but goes back to Plato. In *Gorgias*, Socrates argues that tyrants (who are said to have absolute freedom to do what they want) in fact don't do what they want to do. 'I say, Polus, that tyrants have the least power in their cities. For they do just about nothing they want (*boulontai*) to do, though they certainly do whatever they see (*doxê*) most fit to do' (*Gorg.* 466D8-E2). Proclus refers to this argument in *in Tim.* III 289,16-20: 'the arguments of the *Gorgias* distinguish true will from an apparent *dokêsis*'. See also *in Crat.* 14, p. 5,20-2: '*dokêsis* is often of what is not wanted and not chosen, whereas will is always of what is good'. This Platonic distinction is rejected by Aristotle, *EN* 3.5, 1114a11ff.

259. cf. Aristotle, *EE* 2.11, 1228a11-12: we blame and praise people in the light of the choices they make.

260. This is the fundamental principle of Socratic and Platonic ethics. Olympiodorus calls this 'Platonic dogma' a 'paradox' (*in Gorg.* 190,15ff.). See *Gorg.* 488A3; *Prot.* 345E1; *Meno* 77A-78B; *Resp.* 9, 589C6; *Tim.* 86D2-E1; *Leg.* 9, 860D-E. The last text is quoted by Proclus in his discussion of the problem in *in Remp.* II 355,19ff. See also *De Mal.* ch. 49 and n. 347 in Opsomer-Steel (2003), 127.

261. The expression 'sharp love' is already in Plato (*Leg.* 6, 783A1) to indicate the sexual urge. See also Plutarch, *Coni. Praecepta* 138F7; *Amatorius* 766C8; Callimachus, *Aet.* 75,75. Though the expression in itself is not rare, it is never applied to the love for the good (cf. Plato, *Resp.* 6, 505E: 'the good is that which every soul pursues and for its sake it does all that it does').

262. Animals live without choice (*aproairetôs*). See Proclus, *in Remp.* II 284,13-17 and *in Tim.* III 328,26. Cf. above, n. 62 and 201, where it is said that neither bodies nor corporeal forms of life have a choice.

263. cf. Aristotle, *EE* 2.10, 1226b.

264. On the crossroad between good and evil, see Hesiod, *Op.* 290ff. Yet the most famous exposition of this image is to be found in Xenophon, *Mem.* 2.1.21-34 (Heracles on the crossroad).

265. This is an implicit reference to Plotinus V 3 [49] 3, 44-5: 'sense perception is for us a messenger, but the intellect stands to us as a king'; see also above, ch. 44 and n. 203. In *in Tim.* I 251,15-22 we find the same quote with an explicit reference to 'the great Plotinus'. The image of the intellect as a king is common (already in Plato's *Phil.* 28B), as is the metaphor of the senses as messengers coming from the external world to the soul.

266. On the soul as intermediary being, which can become both extremes through its choice, see *De Decem Dub.* 46,5ff.

267. The term *exousia* means to 'exercise a sovereign authority'. The expression *enexousiazein* is often used for the gods: *in Tim.* II 105,2, 18; *in Parm.* III 804,15-16; *in Alc.* 148,24-9; *in Crat.* 174, p. 98,5; *Theol. Plat.* VI 15, p. 74,18. It is characteristic of tyrannical souls to desire such a sovereign power. Alcibiades too desired to have a licence (*exousia*) to do whatever he wanted (see Plato, *Alc.* 134E8-135A3). According to Proclus he desires to occupy a 'demonic rank' which transcends all life in the world of generation (*in Alc.* 148,19-23).

268. For Proclus, every god has the character of unity. Therefore, providence also is established in unity (see *De Decem Dub.* 10,3) and the divine will is rather 'unitary' than ambivalent. In the gods' will, power and the good are identical, cf. Proclus, *in Tim.* I 373,3ff., Olympiodorus, *in Gorg.* 190,13-14.

269. cf. *Phaedr.* 246C1-2 and above, ch. 24,13-15. According to Proclus the desire to obtain absolute power in politics is a perversion of the desire to govern the whole world together with the gods (*in Alc.* 148,19-149,3).

270. Also Proclus' contemporary Hierocles warns against a misunderstanding of human freedom. In his view, it is not an absolute faculty of self-determination, but a faculty of choice. Cf. Schibli (2002), 356-7 and above, n. 166.

271. See Plotinus VI 8 [39] 2,36-7: 'everything in the sphere of action, even if reason is dominant, is mixed and cannot be fully in our power'.

272. I follow here the conjecture of Westerink (see Philological Appendix). The metaphor of 'colouring' is not uncommon in Neoplatonism, cf. Plotinus VI 7 [38] 22,33-6 ('coloured by the light of the Good'). About evil Proclus says that 'it hides itself taking the colour of the good' (*in Tim.* I 380,1). Westerink quotes

Olympiodorus: 'We say that love, through an excellence of its power, could colour also what is contrary to it' (*in Alc.* 14,23-4).

273. Culmination: *kolophôn*. The same expression is used at the end of *De Decem Dub.* 62,2 (taken from Plutarch, *De Sera Num.* 549D-E). Plato is the first to have used the metaphor of the finishing stone for a final argument, cf. *Euthyd.* 301E1, *Leg.* 2, 673D10; 674C5; *Ep.* 3, 318B4. Cf. also Proclus, *in Tim.* I 69,21; Damascius, *De Princ.* I 5,15. On this culminating problem, see the Introduction, pp. 24-5.

274. On the nature of contingency, see Aristotle, *An. Prior.* 1.13, 32a16ff.; Alexander, *De Fato* 9, p. 175,1ff. with the commentary in Sharples (1983); Proclus, *De Decem Dub.* 1c4.

275. On the interpretation of this difficult text, see the Philological Appendix. Theodore means that even those who do not admit a deterministic interpretation of the world, but accept god's foreknowledge, end up with the conclusion that all contingency disappears.

276. Future contingent events happen in an 'indeterminate way', because the outcome is not predetermined.

277. This seems to be an explanation added by a later scholar. On the views of Stoics and Peripatetics, see the Introduction, pp. 24-5.

278. See *Elem. Theol.* §124, p. 110,10-13: 'Every god knows things divided in an undivided manner, temporal things in a timeless manner, things that are not necessary in a necessary manner, and the mutable immutably, and in general all things in a higher manner than belongs to their order'. See also Dodds' commentary ad loc. on pp. 266-7.

279. cf. *in Remp.* II 234,14-16: 'For also those who construe *parapêgmata* using calculations imitate Nature which has created [the celestial bodies] before calculation and reflection'. As Festugière explains (Festugière (1970), vol. 3, p. 189, n. 5), the *parapêgma* is a stone table that indicates for all the days of the solar year the astronomical positions. Besides (*para*) each indication is a hole in which a nail can be fixed. See Vitruvius, *De Architectura* 9.6.3.

280. *Arrêton, aperiêgêton,* and *aperigraphon* are three terms from negative theology, often used together.

281. The phrase *philê kephalê* literally means 'dear head' and is a Homeric expression (Homer, *Il.* 8.281), already used by Plato; see *Ion* 531D12; *Gorg.* 513C2; *Euthyd.* 293E4; *Phaedr.* 264A8; cf. also Proclus, *in Tim.* I 358,3.

282. Those are indeed the standard arguments against determinism. See Cicero, *De Fato* 27.40: 'neither praise nor blame will be right, neither reward nor punishment'. Already Aristotle made a connection between the assumption of free choice and praise and blame, see Aristotle, *EN* 3.5, 1113b21.

283. sc. Syrianus.

284. cf. Seneca, *Ep. Mor.* 16.4: 'quid mihi prodest philosophia, si fatum est'.

285. As Strobel observes, Proclus alludes here to the famous passage in *Phaedo* (70B10-C2) where Socrates observes that nobody, seeing him talking on immortality just some hours before his death, could say 'that he is babbling and discussing things that do not concern him'. See also *in Parm.* I 656,24-657,5.

286. The *sôrites* is a sophism leading by gradual steps from a true statement to an absurd conclusion, as if adding one grain to one were sufficient to make a 'heap' (*sôros*).

287. On this difficult text, see the Philological Appendix and the Introduction, pp. 25-6. The Stoics were often accused by their opponents of subtleties. For the proverbial expression 'from the same school', see above, n. 128.

Philological Appendix

The translation is based on the Latin translation as edited by Helmut Boese. The often obscure text can be clarified and emended by comparison with the Greek paraphrase of Isaac Sebastocrator (as edited by Daniel Isaac). In the following list I indicate all passages where I deviate from Boese's text or make suggestions to clarify or emend a difficult passage. Many proposed emendations come from Benedikt Strobel (Würzburg), who is preparing an annotated Greek retroversion of the Latin text of the *Tria Opuscula*. 'Read' introduces corrections in the Latin text of Boese; 'understand' proposes Greek terms that may have been in Proclus' original text, but that Moerbeke (or the copyist of his Greek model) misread or misinterpreted; 'sc.' signals the presumable Greek equivalent for a Latin term or phrase, when the paraphrase of Isaac is lacking.

1,1 *conceptus...maturos*, sc. τὰς ὠδῖνας ... ἀκμαίας. I take *maturus* as the translation of ἀκμαῖος, 'ripe, in full bloom, flourishing'. Cf. *in Parm.* IV 935,14 (254,82 Moerbeke), where ἀκμάς is translated as *maturus*. Moerbeke seems to have hesitated on how to translate this term: cf. *in Parm.* III 800,15 (146,7 Moerbeke) *perfectus*, and II 772,9 (124,93 Moerbeke) ἀκμαῖος: *akmealis*. The term ἀκμαῖος is often used in connection with young life, cf. *Theol. Plat.* V 7, p. 27,7-9; 34,19-20. Since only mature animals can give birth, there is a link between 'travail' and 'maturity', cf. Themistius, *Orat.* 356a7: τίκτεται εὐθὺς ἀκμάζοντα ἐκ τῶν ὠδίνων. It is, however, difficult to understand how the 'travail' itself could be 'mature', unless ὠδῖνας is taken here in the sense of 'the fruit of the travail', the insights or concepts.

1,2 *amanti entia speculari*, sc. τῷ φιλοθεάμονι τῶν ὄντων, cf. Plato, *Resp.* V 475E4 (with ἀληθείας). The combination with τῶν ὄντων is characteristic of Proclus, cf. *in Remp.* I 79,1; I 295,30; *De Prov.* 22,14-15.

1,7 *non vane audire*, sc. μὴ παρέργως ἀκοῦσαι, expression often used by Proclus (cf. *in Remp.* I 93,14; 274,20 ;293,26; II 125,19; *in Tim.* II 106,9-10; *Theol. Plat.* IV, p. 31,7); Moerbeke translates παρέργως usually as *preternecessarie*, but see *in Parm.* 310,74: *incurate* ; *uane*

94   Philological Appendix

may be another variation.

1,10   *millesies dicta quidem*, sc. μυριόλεκτά γε [Strobel].

1,10-11   *neque requiem habitura unquam, eo quod anima provocetur*: the expression παῦλαν ἔχειν usually requires a genitive (cf. *Phaedr.* 245C6-7); Moerbeke translated the genitive wrongly as a separative ablative; he also misunderstood προκαλεῖσθαι as a passive; delete comma after *unquam*; this gives the following reconstruction: μηδὲ παῦλαν ἕξοντά ποτε τοῦ τὴν ψυχὴν προκαλεῖσθαι [Strobel].

1,13   *ab illis Plotinicis et Iamblicis*: Boese corrects *Plotinicis et Iamblichicis*, but maybe it is better to correct *Plotinis et Iamblicis* as proposed by Strobel: ἐκείνων τῶν Πλωτίνων καὶ Ἰαμβλίχων. The use of the plural of the personal name to refer to famous individuals (including people similar to them) is attested elsewhere in Proclus. Cf. *in Tim.* II 19,4-5: τοὺς Νικομάχους, τοὺς Μοδεράτους. Same usage in Psellus (*Phil. Minora* II, p. 78,3 and 89,26: Ἰάμβλιχοι καὶ Πλωτῖνοι καὶ Πρόκλοι. Another example is *in Parm.* I 655,6: Proclus mentions the Γοργίαι καὶ Πρωταγόραι and other dialogues of that type (in plural in all manuscripts, but normalised by the editor Cousin, who writes Γοργίας καὶ Πρωταγόρας). This usage is already attested in Plato, cf. *Theaet.* 180E2: Μέλισσοί τε καὶ Παρμενίδαι.

1,12   *cum dederit iam multas directiones*, sc. ὅπου γε δέδωκεν ἤδη πολλὰς εὐθύνας. Εὐθύνη is the public examination after holding an office. The expression διδόναι εὐθύνας means 'to give an account, a justification' to someone, cf. Proclus, *Theol. Plat.* I 8, p. 33,17; *in Parm.* VI 1106,32; *in Eucl.* 15,5. The subject of *dederit* are the plural neutral *millesies dicta*, further explained with the participles *elaborata*, *scripta*, etc. With a plural neutrum the verb can be in singular in Greek. Moerbeke kept in Latin the singular form ("more graeco" as Boese notices).

1,14   *si non grave dicere* could correspond to εἰ μὴ δεινὸν εἰπεῖν ('if it is not dreadful to say so'), cf. Plato, *Phaedr.* 242D4. But this phrase makes no sense in this context. I follow in my translation an excellent conjecture by Strobel: εἴ με δεῖ τοὐμὸν εἰπεῖν, an expression often used by Proclus (cf. *in Remp.* II 101,14; 208,15; 267,18; *Theol. Plat.* III 26, p. 92,20; IV 17, p. 52,3; IV 25, p. 75,22; *in Eucl.* 91,1; *in Parm.* III 826,15, e.a.).

1,18   *sapienter* (σοφῶς): understand σαφῶς Strobel. Cf. Plato, *Tim.* 40D8-9; Proclus, *in Tim.* III 159,22 and *in Remp.* II 236,5.

1,18   *differenter*, sc. διαφερόντως.

2,1   *patienti* [dat. with *tibi*] *dignum indulgentia* [abl. with *dignum*]. The expression συγγνώμης ἄξιον occurs already in Plato, *Resp.* VII 539A6; cf. Proclus, *in Parm.* V 1024,31-33. Put a comma after

Philological Appendix

interrogas (2,2), no full stop.

2,4 *aliasve*: the use of the enclitic *-ve* is not attested in other (published) translations of Moerbeke and it is not in the manuscripts AO. Maybe better to delete.

2,4 *connexiones*: this is the reading of SV, but AO and V *supra lin.* have *funes*; in l. 5 *colligationum* is the reading of V whereas AOS and also V *supra lin.* have *funium*. The term *funes, funium* was probably the original translation, and *connexiones, colligationum* an explication of this term by the translator. See further l. 6 *eirmon (id est connexionem) funium*. The term *funis* 'rope', 'cord', corresponds to σκηνή in 2,6; 27,12; and *De Decem Dub.* 60,21, where we have Isaac's Greek text. This must also be the Greek term corresponding to *funis* in this chapter. It remains puzzling why Moerbeke translated σκηνή as *funis* (a term which could rather be used for εἱρμός). (In his translation of the *Poetics* he uses the transliteration *scene*). Westerink (189) suggests that Moerbeke may have understood σκηνή as σχοινίς (without –s in modern Greek).

2,6-7 *Consequentem generationem*: read *consequentiam generationum*, sc. ἀκολουθίαν γενέσεων (cf. infra 3,4-5 and 39,3-4) [Strobel].

2,7-8 *necessitate inevitabili*, sc. ἀνάγκης ἀπαραβάτου.

2,14 *Irrefragabilem causam*, sc. αἰτίαν ἀναπόδραστον. See Alexander, *De Fato* II, p. 166,2-3: τὴν εἱμαρμένην ὑπολαμβάνουσιν ἀπαράβατόν τινα αἰτίαν εἶναι καὶ ἀναπόδραστον. See Sharples (1983), 126 with further references.

2,8 *solus*, sc. μόνος: understand μόνον [Boese].

3,2 *ianuam*: translator's error (reading θύραν for θήραν); same mistake in the translation of *in Parm.* I 645,14 and I 701,27.

3,5 *necessitate* Boese with A: read *necessitatem* with OSV.

3,7-8 *secundum fatum ... a providentia*: read *secundum fatum ... secundum providentiam* (confusion with *a providentia* in next line) [Strobel].

3,9 *diviniora fato*: read *diuiniore fato*, i.e. more divine than fate [A. Linguiti].

3,17-18 *casus et (...) descensus*. The Latin manuscript V has in the margin πτερορρύησις. Boese supposes that this Greek term, which means the 'moulding or sheding of the wings', corresponds to either *casus* or *descensus*. It is, however, implausible that Moerbeke would have translated this Greek term with *casus* or *descensus*. In *De Mal.* 22,11 he translates the term correctly with *alarum defluentia*. It is better to suppose that he first hesitated how to translate this metaphorical term, left an empty space and had the Greek term in the margin (as was often the case). In the copies of the translation this empty space

96 Philological Appendix

was omitted. I follow Strobel in his reconstruction of the text: ἡ πτῶσις <καὶ ἡ πτερορρύησις> καὶ ἡ (...) κάθοδος. Cf. Plotinus VI 9 [9] 9,23 and Proclus, in Tim. III 43,7.

4,6 *separavit ipsius epistasiam*: understand ἐνεχείρισε αὐτῇ τὴν ἐπιστασίαν. Moerbeke (or his Greek manuscript) probably misread ἐνεχώρισε for ἐνεχείρισε. The verb ἐγχειρίζω means 'undertake, entrust'. For the expression ἐγχειρίζω τὴν ἐπιστασίαν, cf. Iamblichus, De Myst. II 5,7. I also propose to correct *ipsius* into *ipsi* (αὐτῇ). Providence entrusts the care of the corporeal world to the subordinated fate.

4,12 *hebetat*, sc. ἀμβλύνει.

4,18 *intulit*, sc. ἐναπεμόρξατο, as in the margin of V. The verb ἐναπομόργνυμι means 'to wipe off upon, to imprint, to impart'. Proclus uses it in his *Phil. Chald.* 209,2 (preserved by Psellus) for the impression of the passions left upon the pneumatic body. See also Porphyrius, *Sent.* 29, p. 18,10-12 and Iamblichus, *De Myst.* V 3, (201,2), and Psellus, *Phil. Minora* II, p. 19,3-5. As Erler notices, the metaphor goes back to Plato himself who, in the final myth of the *Gorgias*, talks about 'souls full of scars due to crime: the marks branded on (ἐξωμόρξατο) the soul by every evil deed' (*Gorg.* 525A1).

5,12 *queris*: understand ἐζήτεις (conditional irrealis; cf. Isaac ἐζητεῖτο) for ζητεῖς [Strobel].

5,15 *spondere rationem*, sc. ὑπέχειν λόγον (cf. in Parm. I, 695,19) [Strobel].

5,17 *tibi* (σοι): understand μοι [Strobel].

6,7 *quantum ad hoc* (AV): read *quantum ad hec* (with OS).

6,11-12 *et forte satisfacient capientibus nos in presenti de ipsis dubitationibus*: understand καὶ ἴσως ἀποχρήσει <ὁμόσε> χωροῦσιν ἡμῖν ἐν τῷ παρόντι ταῖς περὶ αὐτῶν ἀπορίαις. The expression ὁμόσε χωρεῖν is frequently used in the metaphorical sense of 'coming to issue with' problems, questions. See Proclus, in Tim. I 444,15-16: μετιέναι χρὴ τὴν ἀπορίαν ὁμόσε χωροῦντας. The expression was unknown to Moerbeke, which may explain why he omitted ὁμόσε. The error *nos* for *nobis* may be due to the preceding *capientibus*. For ἴσως ἀποχρήσει, see Plato, Polit. 279B3.

7,1 *indubitanter*, sc. ἀδιστάκτως, 'undisputed, undoubtedly' (cf. in Parm. IV 966,5). But the connection with κοιναὶ ἔννοιαι indicates that we must correct to ἀδιδάκτως (cf. in Eucl. 76,16; Theol. Plat. I 4, p. 22,3 and I 14, p. 64,12; in Parm. IV 954,7; De Decem Dub. 1, 22).

7,6 *quodcumque* (ὁτιοῦν): understand ὁτουοῦν, a genitive depending on *procuratores* [Strobel].

Philological Appendix

7,16   *klosteras*, sc. κλωστῆρας as in the margin of V.

7,17   *dispartitos*, sc. μοιραίους as in the margin of V. Moerbeke understands the adjective μοιραῖος (which means 'fatal') as deriving from μοῖρα (which he usually translates as *pars*): hence, *dispartitos*. Cf. Psellus, *Or. Paneg.* 4.183-5 ed. Dennis: παρὰ τὸν μοιραῖον, ὥς πού τις ἔφησεν, ἀπαγάγοι κλωστῆρα.

7,17   *et momenta partium*: understand καὶ νήματα Μοιρῶν. Strobel supposes that the Latin term *mouimenta* (sic O: *momenta* Boese) stands for κινήματα, which is a corruption for νήματα (the extra κι- may be explained as a diplography καὶ [κι]νήματα). This excellent conjecture is confirmed by many parallels: see footnote 7. Moerbeke does not distinguish between μοῖρα as 'part' and as 'fate' and always translates the term as *pars*.

8,15   *non adhuc*: read <*et*> *non adhuc* [Strobel].

8,19   *prius*: read <*et*> *prius* [Strobel].

9,16   *omnem eternitate*: read *omni* (with V: *omnem* AS *cum* O) *eternitate*, sc. τὸν ἅπαντα αἰῶνα. Moerbeke translates this accusative of duration with an ablative (cf. infra, 20,12) [Strobel].

10,1   *considera a diis*. The Latin may correspond to σκόπει πρὸς θεῶν. The expression πρὸς θεῶν is often used in Plato's dialogues to intensify a question or a reply: 'tell me, answer me by the gods'. This may also be its function here. The context, however, seems to require another interpretation. In ch. 10 Proclus examines the meaning of εἱμαρμένη starting from an analysis of the terms we use for it. We suppose that θεῶν is a corruption of an abbreviated form of ὀνομάτων, and read σκόπει ἀπὸ τῶν ὀνομάτων.

10,4   *autem*, sc. δέ: understand γε.

10,13   *obtentam*, read *obtinentem*, sc. κρατοῦσαν [Strobel].

11,3   *et quecumque*, sc. καὶ ὅσα: understand καθ'ὅσον (cf. Isaac) [Strobel].

11,10   *ei quod*, sc. τῷ: understand τὸ (cf. Isaac) [Boese].

11,11   *conservans*, sc. φυλάττον: understand φυλάττειν (cf. Isaac) [Boese].

11,20   *intelligentialibus*: understand νοεροῖς. Moerbeke had some difficulties in finding Latin equivalent terms for the opposition νοητός-νοερός, which is of great importance in Proclus' theological system. In the *El. Theol.* he translates νοερός as *intellectualis* and νοητός as *intelligibilis*. In other translations (Simplicius, *in Cat.*) he is less careful and uses *intellectualis* also for νοητός. In his last translation (*in Parm.*) he consistently uses *intellectualis* for νοερός, *intelligibilis* or *intelligentialis* for νοητός. The latter term

Philological Appendix

intelligentialis is a new creation of Moerbeke: it appears first in the translation of *De providentia*, where we have two instances with *intelligentialis* corresponding to νοητός in Isaac (13,6 and10). For this passage we have no Greek parallel. It is, however, difficult to translate *intelligentialis* as νοητός. The gods who take care of the universe in the myth of the *Politicus* are Kronos and Zeus, who are undoubtedly 'intellectual gods': see Proclus, *Theol. Plat.* V 6-7. We have to admit that Moerbeke, in this treatise, is not so consistent in his vocabulary as in his later translation of the *in Parm*. Another example is the use of *intellectualis* for νοητός in chapter 14 and in 31,15.

11,22 *nature*, sc. φύσει: one may be tempted to correct and write φύσιν as in *Theol. Plat.* V 32, p. 119,12; but ἐμβλέπω can be constructed with a dative, cf. infra 21,3.

12,1 *isto* (τούτῳ): understand οὕτω [Strobel].

12,6 *illa:* read *illis* (ἐκείνοις)(cf. Isaac τούτοις) [Boese].

12,6 *hec* (ταῦτα): understand πάντα.

12,10 *assequentes* (ἀκολουθοῦσαι): understand ἀκολουθοῦσιν with Isaac [Boese].

12,12 *sub luna*: understand τῶν ὑπὸ σελήνην with Isaac [Boese].

12, 13 *huius* (τῆσδε): understand τῇδε with Isaac [Boese].

illius (ἐκείνου): understand ἐκεῖ with Isaac [Boese].

12,14 *omnibus* (πᾶσι): understand παρά [Strobel].

13,2 *dicimus. Si enim* (λέγομεν εἰ γάρ): understand λέγομεν εἶναι.

13,5 *deinde* (ἔπειτα): add δὲ with Isaac [Boese].

13,9 *providentia fati in se ipsa* (πρόνοια τῆς εἱμαρμένης ἐφ᾽ἑαυτῇ). Isaac has a quite different text τῆς ἀνάγκης ἐφετὸν ἡ πρόνοια (notice that in his compilation ἀνάγκη usually replaces εἱμαρμένη). Boese supposes that *in se ipsa* (ἐφ᾽ἑαυτῇ) is an error for ἐφετόν. The neutrum ἐφετόν, however, remains suspect: it may be an adaptation of the corrupted (ἐφ᾽ἑαυτῇ) by Isaac himself. Strobel proposes as a conjecture ἐπιστατῇ, which I adopt in my translation.

13,13 after *mixtam* the manuscripts have *quidem*: maybe μὲν for τὴν? [Strobel]

13,30 *sub*: understand *et sub* with Isaac [Daniel Isaac].

14,12 *regnant*: read *regnat* [Dudley].

14,4 *quidem*: read *quodam* (τινος) (cf. 10: *diuina aliqua res*) [Helmig].

Philological Appendix 99

16,1   *animam*: read *animarum*.

16,13   *irascens*: add <*et concupiscens*> [Boese].

17,2   *tertiam et plenam*. Boese adopts the reading of A *plenam*. The two other manuscript traditions, V and OS, have *primam*, which seems to be the authentic reading (see my note 68). *Tertiam et primam* is at first odd, and one understands why *plenam* may have seemed a better reading and why Isaac Sebastocrator skipped this phrase altogether.

17,3   *corrigentem aut*: read *aut corrigentem* [Boese].

17,7   *immensuratum ens motu:* ἄμετρον ὂν τῆς κινήσεως. The participle *ens* is lacking in Isaac's compilation. Because of this *ens* Moerbeke could not understand κινήσεως as a genitive with ἄμετρον, and translated it as an ablative. The ὂν may be a simple dittography.

17,8   *corde*: understand with Homer κραδίη for κραδίῃ [Boese].

17,11   *meliorata* (ἀμεινομένη?): understand with Isaac ἀμυνομένη cf; also 25,18 and 37,8 [Boese].

17,21   *novit* (οἶδεν): understand εἶδεν with Plato and Isaac [Boese].

17,24   *sequestratur*: add ἃς with Isaac [Boese].

18,1   *video* (ὁρῶ) understand ὅρα [Strobel].

18,1-2 *ea...rationali anima*: comparative ablative in Moerbeke's translation, but in fact a subject genitive with κίνησιν [Strobel].

18,23   *inapplicabiles*: ὁδοὶ Isaac. One needs, however, an adjective corresponding to καθαρτικαί. I propose ἀναγωγοί. Both terms or often used together to describe the role of mathematics in the educational process: see *in Tim.* I 38,10; 212,20; and *in Eucl.* 29,26-27. Ἀνάγειν εἰς (πρὸς) περιωπήν is often found in Proclus, see *in Remp.* I 77,10; 166,13; *in Alc.* 19,17 and 21,1; *Theol. Plat.* IV 4,p. 18,7; V 8, p. 29,23; IV 13, p. 44,8. It is difficult to explain how ἀναγωγοί could have been translated as *inapplicabiles*.

        divinam (θείαν): understand θείων (cf. *in Remp.* I 77,11).

19,2   *recurrens* (ἀναδραμὼν Isaac): understand ἀνάδραμε (cf. *in Parm.* VI 1120,23).

19,21-22 *eam que...prolocuta est*: understand ἧς φθεγγομένης [Strobel].

19, 22 *et audisse*: understand φασὶν ἀκοῦσαι [Strobel].

19,24   *divine partis*, sc. θεόμοιρος [Strobel].

20,7   *quantum* (ὅσον): ὥσπερ τινῶν Isaac, ὥς τινων Strobel.

21, 3	*nature*: cf. supra ad 11,22.
21,4	*fato: fatum* corr. Cousin, τὴν εἱμαρμένην Psellus, θειμαρμένον coni. des Places.
21,5	*cuius finis*....: The Latin manuscripts all have a lacuna after *finis*: Kroll (50, n. 1) adds <οὐδέν>; Lewy (1956), 266 n. 23 conjectures Ἅιδης as missing noun.
21,14	*nostra* (ἡμῶν): understand ἡμᾶς with Isaac [Boese].
21, 15	*autem*: understand δὴ [Strobel].
21,16	*fient*: read *aiunt* (φασί) [Strobel].
22, 8	*quecumque*: add πρῴην with Isaac and the Latin manuscript V [Boese].
22,9-17	for the reconstruction and interpretation of this text, I follow Westerink.
22,12	*forte*: read *fore* (ἔσεσθαι) with V [Strobel].
22,14	*insidentibus* (ὀχουμένων): understand οἰχομένων with Isaac [Boese].
22,16	*effectibus*: read *affectibus* (τραυμάτων Isaac) [Westerink].
23,3	*deorsum*: sc. τῶν κάτω Boese, gen. absolutus [Westerink].
23,7	after *obtinentes* there may be a lacuna. We expect something parallel to *non nos sumus qui dicimus sed est concupiscentie verbum*. But maybe we have to add a similar phrase mentally.
23,7-8	*hoc*: read *huius* (O: hoc ASV), sc. ταύτης [Strobel].
23,15	*utique* (που): understand ποῦ with Isaac [Strobel].
23,15	add καὶ before *quomodo* with Isaac [Strobel].
23,16	*in quibus divino: divino* (τῷ θείῳ) seems superfluous; it may be a readers' note added supra lineam.
24,10	*a qua* (ἀφ᾽ἧς): ἀφ᾽οὗ (sc. *deo*) Isaac; understand ἀφ᾽ὧν (sc. *diis*) [Strobel].
25,18	*melioratus* (ἀμεινόμενος?): understand ἀμυνόμενος with Isaac (cf. supra 17,11; infra 37,8) [Boese].
25,19	*nobis*: read *vobis* [Boese].
26,7	*autem*: understand μὲν with Isaac [Boese].
26,10	*talia* (τοιαῦτα): understand τοσαῦτα [Strobel].
27,4	*num igitur*: understand οὐκοῦν and drop question mark after

veritatem (6).

27,4 ff. *aliam quidem*.... Strobel connects this *aliam quidem* with *hac autem tanta ente alteram* in 28,1. He supposes that Proclus abandoned the original planned construction (*alteram autem*) because of the long digression in 27,6-12. It is the simplest solution, even if not fully convincing. The *aliam quidem* remains problematic.

28,1 *tanta* (τοσαύτης): understand τοιαύτης [Strobel].

29,1 *tertiam...dic me dicere*, sc. τρίτην φάθι με λέγειν: cf. *Phil.* 26D7 [Strobel].

30,23 *fatalem connexuit*, sc. οἱ μοῖραν ἐδαίσατο (cf. οἱμοιραν ἐδαισατο mg. V) [Westerink].

31,4 *autem*: understand τε.

31,6 *ipsam* A Boese: read *ipsum* with OSV; replace double point after *diuulgant* by comma.

31,6 *aiunt* is an interjection qualifying 'the one of the soul': 'as they say'.

31,7 *excitantem et coaptantem*. The two participles must be connected, just as *assequentem* (5), to *uolo te* (2). Maybe the two participles (ἀνεγείραντα...συνάψαντα) are corruptions of infinitive aorist forms: ἀξιῶ σε...ἑπόμενον...ἀνεγεῖραι...συνάψαι.

31,11 *quo adiaciens le unum* (ᾧ ἐπιβάλλουσα τὸ ἕν). *Quo* corresponds to a dative pronoun, as is clear from Isaac (ᾧ). But what is its antecedent? Isaac connects ᾧ with the ἕν (*unum*) of l. 9. Strobel corrects the preceding *illa* (ἐκεῖνα) into ἐκεῖνο and understands *adiaciens* (ἐπιβάλλουσα) transitive and construes '*unum*' as its direct object: (cf. *De Decem Dub.* 5,7: *omnibus iniciens le unum*). I prefer to follow Isaac. *Le unum* may have been added by the translator to identify the floating *quo*.

31,12 *cognitionibus*: understand ταῖς κάτω γνώσεσι (cf. ταῖς καταγνώσεσι mg. A) [Westerink].

32,2 *sibi ipsi* (ἑαυτῷ): understand ἑαυτὸν with Isaac [Strobel].

32,7 *hec*: read *hoc* [Strobel].

33,6 *frivolum* (φλαῦρον): understand φλύαρον [Strobel].

33,6-7 *sed obtinet celestium partium sola ad singula eorum que fiunt factionem*, sc. ἀλλὰ κρατεῖν τὴν τῶν οὐρανίων Μοιρῶν μόνην εἰς ἕκαστα τῶν γιγνομένων ποίησιν. One could construe this phrase as depending on *argumentum eius quod* (5), which, however, would require the conjunctive mode *obtineat* (*obtinet* AS: *oportet* O *opera et* V), corresponding to *sit* (6). Westerink proposes to read *operatio* for *partium* and to correct *singula eorum* into *singulorum*. But *partium* stands for Μοιρῶν (cf. Daniel Isaac). It is better to suppose that Moerbeke construed ποίησιν (factionem) erroneously with εἰς (ad) and did not notice that it is an accusative as subject of the infinitive κρατεῖν (not an accusative of object, as Erler supposes; for κρατεῖν is construed with genitive). Moerbeke should have translated sed obtineat ... factio.

33,9-10   ad illam causam, scilicet necessitatem, transferimus pro electione. Moerbeke erroneously understood (or read) εἰς ἐκείνην τὴν αἰτίαν 'towards that cause' and added scilicet necessitatem to explain what cause is meant. But one should construe causam transferimus ad illam (sc. the factio of the celestial Moirai). Cf. Alexander, De Fato VII, p. 171,28-172,1: ἐπὶ τὴν εἱμαρμένην ἀφ'αὐτῶν τὴν αἰτίαν τῶν κακῶν μεταφέροντας and Proclus, in Remp. II 260,7-8 [Strobel].

34,5-6   propter quandam filautiam, id est amorem sui, malum et inconvenientem. Inconveniens is usually a translation of ἄτοπος. I propose to correct ἄτοπον into ἄλογον, which is often used in connection with φιλαυτία. Cf. Porphyrius, De Abstinentia III 2,15.

34,7   add <et> before quem [Boese].

34,13   rerum (πραγμάτων): understand πρακτῶν with Isaac [Boese].

34,19   post deum (μετὰ θεόν): understand μετὰ θεοῦ as in Plato (cf. De Decem Dub. 51,10 cum diis) [Strobel].

34,20   nostrum (ἡμέτερον): understand ἡμερώτερον with Plato [Boese].

34,23   fatum: read fat<at>um (cf. De Decem Dub. 55,28: tempora fatata) [Strobel].

34,28   sed (ἀλλὰ): understand ἅμα [Strobel].

34,33   excedentium, sc. χορευουσῶν Isaac.

35,2   solo: understand sola (μόνης) with Isaac [Cousin/Boese].

35,16   verere: understand ἔνδυθι (in margine V) [Westerink].

35,17   institit: 'sing. verbi ad neutr. plur. (responsa) e textu Gr. servavit Guilelmus; lege: institerunt' [Boese].

36,7   electivum: add aut (ἢ).

37,6   unde quidem igitur (ὅθεν μὲν οὖν): understand ὅθεν σὺ μὲν [Strobel].

37,8   melior factus (ἀμεινόμενος?) pro ἀμυνόμενος (cf. also 17,11 and 25,18) [Boese].

37,9   ex motu solo: read ex motu celi.

37,18   poni: erroneously for τίθεσθαι (medium).

Philological Appendix

37,18 *et²*: understand εἰς [Westerink] or πρός (cf. *in Alc.* 144,10).

38,2 *sacrorum* (ἱερῶν): ἱερέων coni. Daniel Isaac. Cf. Iamblichus, *De Myst.* II 11,12; V 14,7; Proclus, *in Remp.* I 78,18 (where the same corruption occurs); see also infra 39,2. Isaac rewrites the expression as ἱερατικήν.

et hoc: read *et hos* (sc. *sacerdotes*) [Daniel Isaac].

38,4 *servire*: understand ἱκετείας γίγνεσθαι with Isaac [Boese]. Moerbeke probably read οἰκετείας for ἱκετείας (Thillet), hence his translation *servire*.

38,5 *omnino* (πάντως): understand πάντας with Isaac [Boese].

38,9 *occurrere* (ἀπαντήσεσθαι): understand ἀπαντήσεται [Strobel].

38,10 *dividi*: understand συνδιαιρεῖσθαι with Isaac [Boese].

39,2 *sacrorum* (ἱερῶν): understand ἱερέων (cf. 38,2).

39,9 *talibus* (τοιούτων): understand ποιούντων with Isaac [Boese].

39,16 *verberibus* (μάστιξιν?): understand πλάστιγξιν with Isaac (cf. marginal note in manuscript V) [Boese].

40,1 *Hiis igitur consequenter, ut michi uideris ipse, gubernat* [...]. Much seems to be corrupted in this initial phrase. One expects an infinitive such as 'declare' or 'establish' after *uideris* (δοκεῖς). Maybe the pronoun *ipse* (αὐτός) originally was a part of a verb now lost. Further, a subject is lacking before *gubernat*, maybe 'the world soul'. Finally, one has to correct *gubernat* (κυβερνᾷ) in *gubernare* (κυβερνᾶν), since an infinitive is needed, as the rest of the sentence is in indirect speech.

40,3 *aere* (ἀέρος): understand *ethere* αἰθέρος cf. ch. 42 [Strobel].

41,1 The first sentence is the conclusion of the previous chapter [Westerink].

41,3-4 *earum que secundum eruditionem viarum*, sc. τῶν κατὰ παίδευσιν ὁδῶν, an expression taken from *Tim.* 53C2.

41,6 *huius* (ταύτης): understand ταύτας [Strobel].

42,15 *a deo tradita*, sc. θεοπαράδοτα: this term is not attested before Proclus who uses it for the Chaldaean Oracles (six other references); through him it became a favourite term of Ps.-Dionysius (18 instances).

42,18 *specula* (θέας): understand θεᾶς (*dea*) [Cousin/Boese].

42,21 *quandoque* (ποτε): understand τότε [Lewy].

43,1	*et:* understand ἢ with Isaac [Boese].
43,8	*hec*: read *hee* (αἱ Isaac) [Boese].
43,9	*ait* (φησιν): understand φασιν (cf. διδάσκουσι Isaac) [Boese].
43,10	*que aliquod*: Boese suggests *que quid*, which corresponds to τὰ τί in Isaac. I propose to read τὸ <ὅ>τι; cf. Arist., *Metaph.* 1.1, 981a28-9 and *An. Post.* 1.13, 79a3 ff.
44,3	*separabilis*: read *inseparabilis* (cf. ἀχώριστον Isaac) [Cousin/Boese].
44,4	*conversa ... non contingit dicere*: οὐκ ἐνδέχεται στραφῆναι πρὸς ἑαυτὴν καὶ λογίσασθαι Isaac. This is a rather free paraphrase of a text that probably was already corrupt. Following Isaac one could understand *conuersa* as στραφῆναι, write *ipsam* instead of *ipsa*, and add *et* before *dicere*. But maybe it is better to correct *conuersa* and suppose Proclus originally wrote <ἀνεπί>στροφον.
44,6	*passionem nuntiavit*: read *passio enuntiavit* (cf. Isaac) [Thillet, Boese].
45,8-9	*intellectum autem senilem presidem statuenti intellectualis prudentis iudicii conceptus convenire*. The genitive adjective *intellectualis* (νοερᾶς) duplicates *prudentis*. Strobel proposes to interpret it as νοερὰς and connect it with *conceptus* (ἐννοίας). I follow him in my translation. One may doubt, however, whether *conceptus* corresponds here to ἔννοιαι. The combination νοεραὶ ἔννοιαι never occurs in Proclus (but see *Or. Chald.* fr. 37,14). Or should we suppose νοερὰς ... ἐπιβολάς, an expression that occurs frequently in Proclus. For *conceptus* as a translation of ἐπιβολή, cf. *in Parm.* III 801,14 (146,24 Moerbeke). The connection between ἐπιβολή and κρίσις is made in *in Remp.* I 110,17.
45,18	*sibi et*: read *sibimet* [Strobel].
46,11	*non enim*: add δεῖ [Strobel].
46,13	*accepta* (ἀποδεδεγμένα): understand ἀποδεδειγμένα [Van Campe].
46,46	*rursum evidenter dicta fabulari*, sc. αὖτις ἀριζήλως εἰρημένα μυθολογεύειν [Westerink].
47,2	*delectabili:* read *delectari* (ἥδεσθαι) (cf. Plotinus IV 7 [2] 19,2) [Strobel].
47,8	*aliud* (ἄλλο): understand ἄλλα [Strobel].
48,2-6	Change punctation. *Sed que post hec scribis dubitans?* is a rhetorical question, followed by the tentative opinion of the questioner: *Videris utique mihi ... audiens ... dubitare ...* The dashes introduced by Boese to indicate a parenthetic clause are not needed.

Philological Appendix

48,7	*cointelligere*: add <ὅτι> [Strobel].
48,9-10	*eius quod non in nobis*: τοῦ μὴ <εἶναι τὸ> ἐφ᾽ἡμῖν [Strobel].
49,3	*sumens* (λαβοῦσα): understand λαχοῦσα with Isaac [Boese].
	quas: understand ὧν with Isaac [Boese].
49,8	*mediocriter* (μετρίως): understand μετρίας [Strobel].
49,18	*unius*: μιᾶς, sc. ἐνεργείας [Linguiti].
50,4	*determinat* (διορίζει): read *determinans* (διορίζων) [Strobel].
50,5	*hanc* (ταύτην): understand αὐτήν [Strobel].
50,12	*pigritie coegit et iudicium et sententiam*, sc. νοθείας ὑπέσχε καὶ κρίσιν καὶ ψῆφον [Westerink].
51, 12	*ignorabit* (ἀγνοοίη): understand γνοίη with Isaac [Boese].
51,14	*que* (ἃ): understand ὃ with Isaac [Boese].
51,15-16	*scientium et eorum qui*: modify into singular form with Isaac (τοῦ εἰδότος καὶ τοῦ) [Strobel].
52,1-2	*Sapiens…sciens*: this sentence is the conclusion of the previous argument.
52,1	*cognoscet*: add <*se ipsum*> (cf. 51,7-8).
52,3	*competens*: one expects rather *competit* (ἐπιβάλλει?).
52,8-9	*quam… quam…*: indirect questions depending on a lost verb. The distinction between the different levels of knowledge of the soul, both when connected and when liberated from the body, is discussed extensively in chs 27-32. What follows here, is a summary of the doctrine of the five levels of the soul. One expects an expression referring to that earlier discussion. I propose to add after *vinculo* <διὰ τῶν ἔμπροσθεν διώρισται> (see l. 10). Strobel understands with Isaac the interrogative pronouns as indefinite.
52,9	*quas*: τινὰς here we need an indefinite pronoun.
52,10	after *cognitiones* add ἐπιστήμας with Isaac [Boese].
52,10	*ponet* (θήσεται): who? The soul? Plato quoted before? Or an indefinite 'one'? But a future makes no sense here. I propose to correct into εἴρηται.
52,12	*deificam*: ἔνθεον is probably a Christian adaptation by Isaac. Proclus probably wrote θεοποιόν.
52,13	*hac*: understand τῇδε with Isaac [Boese].

Philological Appendix

53,5 — *licet et aliis melioratis dubitationem dicere*. Here again *melioratis* stands for ἀμυνομένοις (see supra 17,11; 25,18; 37,8). Strobel proposes another correction: ἄλλως (for ἄλλοις).

53,8 — *idem* : understand < κατὰ > ταὐτόν [Strobel].

53,12-13 — *Plotinum illum, Iamblichum, equivocum tibi*, sc. τὸν Πλωτῖνον ἐκεῖνον, τὸν Ἰάμβλιχον, τὸν ὁμώνυμόν σοι. Notice the beautiful allusion to Demosthenes, *Olynth.* 3, 21: τὸν Ἀριστείδην ἐκεῖνον, τὸν Νικίαν, τὸν ὁμώνυμον ἐμαυτῷ [Strobel].

53,16 — *salvatus*: ἐξάντης (sic margine A), 'free from danger': a rare term, but already in Plato, *Phaedr.* 244E2; Hermias in his Commentary feels the need to explain it (*in Phaedr.* 97,25-7). Proclus uses the term once in *in Remp.* II 6,25. The Latin *occursor* is probably a first attempt to translate this rare Greek term.

54,2 — *sed*: <ad inquisitionem> adds Cousin.

54,2-3 — *argumenta, sicut eius quod non sit le in nobis*: read *sint* for *sicut* (*sint* A: *sit* O *sicut* SV) and understand τεκμήρια εἶναι τοῦ μὴ εἶναι τὸ ἐφ᾽ἡμῖν [Westerink].

54,4 — *sit, magis*: read *sit magis,*

55,8-9 — *Et ego valde letor ad tales dubitationes videns generosum adventicium, qui sepe iubeo*. This sentence makes no senses until one realises that the term *adventicium*, which in Moerbeke's translations often corresponds to the adjective ἐπίκτητος here stands for the philosopher with the name of Ἐπίκτητος. The Stoic philosopher Epictetus was not known in the Latin Middle Ages: therefore it is not surprising that Moerbeke failed to translate this personal name, making it *adventicium*. That we have here a reference to Epictetus is also clear from what follows in this chapter: a paraphrase of the first paragraphs of the *Enchiridion*, a text popular also in the Neoplatonic school, as is evident from the beautiful commentary written by Simplicius. The term *generosus* stands for γενναῖος, a term often used by Proclus to introduce a famous philosopher: Amelius (*in Remp.* II 275,30; *Theol. Plat.* V 5, p. 23,9; *in Tim.* I 309,21; 336,20); Heraclitus (*in Alc.* 256,1; *in Tim.* I 102,25; 174,12); Theodore of Asine (*in Tim.* II 142,14). Because Moerbeke did not understand the reference, he also made an error in the translation of what follows: *qui sepe iubeo* (παρακελευόμενος) should be corrected into *qui sepe iubet* (παρακελευόμενον). This is the complete retroversion: καὶ ἐγὼ πάνυ ἄγαμαι εἰς τὰς τοιαύτας ἀπορίας βλέπων τὸν γενναῖον Ἐπίκτητον πολλάκις παρακελευόμενον. [After the completion of the translation I discovered that the same correction had already been proposed independently by Jean Pierre Schneider in his article "Une mention

Philological Appendix

(cachée) d'Epictète chez Proclus (Procl. De prov. 55,5-18 [Boese])", in *Interpretation und Argument*, hrsg. von H. Linneweber-Lammerskitten und G. Mohr, Köningshausen und Neumann, Würzburg, 2002, pp. 121-8].

55,11   *ut non et facta*: read *ut non et <non> facta* [Strobel].

55,17   *que <non> in nobis* [Cousin].

55,21   *quod dixi viris*, sc. οὓς ἔλεγον ἀνδράσι cf. *Tim.* 25E3.

55,22   *solvunt*: translation of λύουσι which Moerbeke understood as the third person plural form of the verb λύω. We interpret it as a dative plural of the participle and connect it with ἀνδράσι.

56,2   *dubitas* (ἀπορεῖς): understand ἀπορεῖν [Strobel].

57,3   *considera...quam vera dico*: *quam* translates ἤ which makes no sense here. Better to correct ἤ into εἰ (similar phrase in *Meno* 81B2-3 and *Hippias maior* 302E3) [Strobel].

57,9   *electionem* (προαίρεσιν): read *electivam* (προαιρετικήν): cf. infra l. 19 (*electivam*).

58,4   *vivere illa*: Cousin corrected *illa* into *illam* (i.e. the irrational power: cf. *in Tim.* III 328,26); but *illa* can stand for 'the irrational animals'; or is *illa* a corruption for *animalia* (*a'lia*)?

60,10   *sit* (ᾖ): understand ἦν [Strobel].

61,5   *eligentem*: maybe better *electivam*.

61,5   *efficientibus* (ἀποτελοῦσι): The Latin ablative could be connected with *appetibilibus*: 'the desirable things ... which make the elective soul of such a character'. Maybe it is better to correct ἀποτελοῦσι into ἀπετέλεσας ('you made') corresponding to *existimasti* in l. 2. We then need a semi-colon after *desiderat* (4). This is indeed how I have translated.

61,7   *commixta*: add <*est*>.

61,10   *utentes*: in the margin of V one reads χρώσαντες. As Westerink observes, this is the good reading, which Moerbeke wrongly translated as *utentes*, taking the term for χρήσαντες.

62,6-7   *Et consueuit etiam hoc ponentibus non omnia coacta esse*: read *conuenit* (συμβαίνει) for *consueuit* (which makes no sense here: εἴωθε requires a verb such as λέγειν) and interpret: καὶ συμβαίνει καὶ τοῦτο τοῖς τιθεμένοις μὴ πάντα ἠναγκάσθαι. For a parallel of the construction, see *Theol. Plat.* II 1, p. 9,4-5.

63,10   *corporum*: read *corporeorum* (σωματικῶν) [Strobel].

65,1-2   *fixit huic eventum*: ἐπάγεται τούτῳ ἡ ἔκβασις [Isaac]. This is

Philological Appendix

probably a free adaptation of Isaac. Moerbeke recognized a form of πήγνυμι. Strobel proposes πέπηγε (perfectum with passive sense) and supposes that Moerbeke read πέπηχε and translated it as an active verb.

65,3   *dans* (διδούς): understand δίδου [Strobel], or should we prefer δοτέον as proposed by Daniel Isaac (*dandum*)?

65,5   *illa* (ἐκείνη): understand ἐκεῖ with Isaac [Boese].

65,9-10   replace question mark by comma after *precognitione*; put question mark after *incircumscriptibile*.

65,10   *non tamquam* (οὐχ ὡς): introducing another rhetorical question as an answer to the first (cf. *in Alc.* 55,10-15 and *in Parm.* VI 1051,21-24); a better translation would have been *non quod* [Westerink].

66, 3   *provocationibus*, sc. προτροπῶν [Westerink].

66,13-15   *Eum autem qui ex superbia cumulum et laqueum et omnem qui ex eodem illis exercitio aiunt stultiloquum, inclino tibi, non adventicie michi.*

This conclusion poses many problems of interpretation. I propose the following retroversion (partially inspired by Strobel): τὴν δὲ ἐκ τῆς Στοᾶς σωρείτην καὶ παγίδα καὶ πάντα τὸν ἐκ τοῦ αὐτοῦ τούτοις γυμνασίου, φασί, στρουθῶν φλήναφον ἐπισκήπτω σοι μή μοι ἐπεισάγειν. To justify this retroversion, we may start from the phrase στρουθῶν φλήναφον which is preserved in the margin of the Latin manuscript V (στρουθὸν φλαναφον). The term φλήναφον is used for 'idle talk, nonsense'. The combination with στρουθῶν does not occur elsewhere, though Proclus seems to consider it a common expression (φασί). However, the *aiunt* may also qualify the preceding phrase, which comes from *Gorg.* 493D5-6 (already quoted in ch. 28, see n. 128 of the translation).

Cumulus could be a translation of σωρός (heap), but in this context probably stands for σωρείτης, a complicated chain of arguments, for which the Stoics were often criticized by their opponents (See Cicero, *Acad.* II 16,49). What about *ex superbia*? Moerbeke translates τῦφος as *superbia* in *in Parm.* I 686,16. Assuming that Moerbeke has read in his Greek manuscript ἐκ τύφου, Strobel conjectures ἔκτυφον. The meaning 'deluding' goes well in the context, the term ἔκτυφος, however, is extremely rare. Chr. Helmig suggests to read ἐκ τῆς Στοᾶς because of the reference 'from the same school as those (τούτοις)', which follows. But how to explain the corruption of *stoa* into *superbia*? Anyway, the context makes clear that Proclus is attacking the subtleties of the Stoic school.

The following term *laqueus* points in the same direction. For the metaphor of 'trap' or 'snare' is sometimes used for Stoic arguments

Philological Appendix

in polemical texts. Thus, Aulus Gellius tells about an arrogant young man, a student of Stoic philosophy, who was accustomed to talk endlessly on philosophical matters. 'As he spoke, he rattled off unfamiliar terms, the catchwords of syllogisms and dialectical tricks (*dialecticarum laqueis*), declaring that no one but he could unravel the "master", the "resting" and the "heap" (σωρείτας) arguments and other riddles of the kind.' (*Noctes atticae*, I 2,4, transl. J.Rolfe) Already Cicero observed: 'Stoici vero nostri disputationum suarum atque interrogationum laqueis te inretitum tenerent.' (*De oratore* I 42) Cf. also *Tusc. Disp.* V 27,76 'ut iam a laqueis Stoicorum, quibus usum me pluribus quam soleo intellego, recedamus.'

The final clause is again a puzzle: ἐπεισάγειν is a conjecture (inspired by Strobel) for *adventicie* (ἐπεισάκτως). *Inclino* could be a translation of ἐπικύπτω, which itself may be a corruption of ἐπισκήπτω.

Select Bibliography

1. Editions and translations of the *Tria Opuscula* and related texts

1.1. Proclus

For a recent survey of editions, translations, and secondary literature on Proclus see C. Steel *et al.*, *Proclus: Fifteen Years of Research (1990-2004). An Annotated Bibliography*, Göttingen, 2005.

Procli philosophi Platonici opera inedita quae primus olim e codd. mss. Parisinis Italicisque vulgaverat nunc secundis curis emendavit et auxit Victor Cousin, Parisiis, 1864 [= Frankfurt am Main, 1962].

Procli Diadochi Tria Opuscula (De providentia, libertate, malo). Latine Guilelmo de Moerbeka vertente et Graece ex Isaacii Sebastocratoris aliorumque scriptis collecta, edidit Helmut Boese (Quellen und Studien zur Geschichte der Philosophie, 1), Berolini, 1960.

Proclus. Trois études sur la Providence, I, *Dix problèmes concernant la Providence*. Texte établi et traduit par Daniel Isaac (Collection des Universités de France), Paris, 1977.

Proklos Diadochos. Über die Existenz des Bösen. Übersetzt und erläutert von Michael Erler (Beiträge zur klassischen Philologie, 102), Meisenheim am Glan, 1978.

Proclus. Trois études sur la Providence, II, *Providence, fatalité, liberté*. Texte établi et traduit par Daniel Isaac (Collection des Universités de France), Paris, 1979.

Proclus. Trois études sur la Providence, III, *De l'existence du mal*. Texte établi et traduit par Daniel Isaac, avec une note additionnelle par Carlos Steel (Collection des Universités de France), Paris, 1982.

Proklos Diadochos. Über die Vorsehung, das Schicksal und den freien Willen an Theodoros, den Ingenieur (Mechaniker). Nach Vorarbeiten von Theo Borger, übersetzt und erläutert von Michael Erler (Beiträge zur klassischen Philologie, 121), Meisenheim am Glan, 1980.

Proclo. Tria Opuscula. Provvidenza, libertà, male. Dieci questioni sulla provvidenza. Lettera all'inventore Teodoro sulla provvidenza, il fato è ciò che è sotto il potere dell'uomo. Sull'esistenza del male. Introduzione, traduzione, note e apparati di Francesco D. Paparella; testo greco a cura di Alberto Bellanti (Il Pensiero Occidentale), Milano, 2004.

Procli Diadochi in primum Euclidis Elementorum librum commentarii, ex recognitione Godofredi Friedlein (Bibliotheca scriptorum Graecorum et Romanorum Teubneriana), Lipsiae, 1873.

Procli Diadochi in Platonis Rem Publicam commentarii, edidit Guilelmus Kroll (Bibliotheca scriptorum Graecorum et Romanorum Teubneriana), Lipsiae, vol. I, 1899; vol. II, 1901.

Proclus. Commentaire sur la République. Traduction et notes par A.J. Festugière, tomes I-III, Paris, 1970.
Procli Diadochi in Platonis Timaeum commentaria, edidit Ernestus Diehl (Bibliotheca scriptorum Graecorum et Romanorum Teubneriana), Lipsiae, vol. I, 1903; vol. II, 1904; vol. III, 1906.
Proclus. Commentaire sur le Timée. Traduction et notes par A.J. Festugière, tomes I-V, Paris, 1966-8.
Procli Diadochi in Platonis Cratylum commentaria, edidit Georgius Pasquali (Bibliotheca scriptorum Graecorum et Romanorum Teubneriana), Lipsiae, 1908.
Proclus. The Elements of Theology. A Revised Text with Translation, Introduction and Commentary by E.R. Dodds, 2nd edn, Oxford, 1963.
Proclus. Théologie platonicienne. Texte établi et traduit par H.D. Saffrey et L.G. Westerink (Collection des Universités de France), Paris, *Livre I*, 1968; *Livre II*, 1974; *Livre III*, 1978; *Livre IV*, 1981; *Livre V*, 1987; *Livre VI. Index général*, 1997.
Proclus. Sur le Premier Alcibiade de Platon. Texte établi et traduit par A.-Ph. Segonds (Collection des Universités de France), Paris, tome I, 1985; tome II, 1986.
Proclus. Commentaire sur le Parménide de Platon. Traduction de Guillaume de Moerbeke. Édition critique par Carlos Steel (Ancient and Medieval Philosophy, De Wulf-Mansion Centre, Series 1, 3; 4), Leuven, tome I, *Livres I-IV*, 1982; tome II, *Livres V-VII*, 1985.
Proclus' Commentary on Plato's Parmenides. Translated by Glenn R. Morrow and John M. Dillon, with Introduction and Notes by John M. Dillon, Princeton, 1987.
Procli In Platonis Parmenidem Commentaria, edidit Carlos Steel, tomus I, libros I-III continens: recognoverunt Carlos Steel, Caroline Macé, Pieter d'Hoine (Scriptorum classicorum bibliotheca Oxoniensis), Oxford, 2007. This new edition has been used for references to Books 1-3.

1.2. Calcidius
Timaeus a Calcidio translatus commentarioque instructus, edidit J.H. Waszink, in societatem operis coniuncto P.J. Jensen (Corpus Platonicum Medii Aevi, Plato Latinus, 4), editio altera, London-Leiden, 1975.

1.3. Chaldean Oracles
Oracles Chaldaïques, avec un choix de commentaires anciens. Texte établi et traduit par Édouard des Places (Collection des Universités de France), Paris, 1971.
The Chaldean Oracles. Text, Translation, and Commentary by Ruth Majercik (Studies in Greek and Roman Religion, 5), Leiden-New York-København, 1989.

1.4. Damascius
Damascius. *Traité sur les premiers principes.* Texte établi par L.G. Westerink et traduit par J. Combès (Collection des Universités de France), 3 vols, Paris, 1986-91.
Damascius. *Commentaire du Parménide de Platon.* Texte établi par L.G. Westerink et traduit par J. Combès (Collection des Universités de France), 4 vols, Paris, 1997-2003.

1.5. Gregory of Nyssa
Gregory of Nyssa, *Letter to Macedonius (On Fate).* Edited by J.A. McDonough, in *Gregorii Nysseni Opera dogmatica minora*, Pars II, Leiden, 1987, 27-63.

1.6. Isaak Sebastokrator
Isaak Sebastokrator. Zehn Aporien über die Vorsehung. Herausgegeben von Johannes Dornseiff (Beiträge zur klassischen Philologie, 19), Meisenheim am Glan, 1966.
Isaak Sebastokrator. ΠΕΡΙ ΤΗΣ ΤΩΝ ΚΑΚΩΝ ΥΠΟΣΤΑΣΕΩΣ (De malorum subsistentia). Herausgegeben von James J. Rizzo (Beiträge zur klassischen Philologie, 42), Meisenheim am Glan, 1971.
Isaak Sebastokrator. Uber Vorsehung und Schicksel. Herausgegeben von Michael Erler (Beiträge zur klassischen Philologie, 111), Meisenheim am Glan, 1979.

1.7. Nemesius
Nemesii Emeseni De natura hominis, edidit Moreno Morani (Bibliotheca scriptorum Graecorum et Romanorum Teubneriana), Leipzig, 1987.

1.8. Marinus
Marinus, Proclus ou Sur le bonheur. Texte établi, traduit et annoté par H.D. Saffrey et A.-P. Segonds, avec la collaboration de C. Luna (Collection des Universités de France), Paris, 2001.

1.9. Plato
Platonis opera recognovit brevique adnotatione critica instruxit Ioannes Burnet (Scriptorum classicorum bibliotheca Oxoniensis), 5 vols, Oxford, 1900-7.
The Collected Dialogues of Plato, Including the Letters. Edited by Edith Hamilton and Huntington Cairns (Bollingen Series, 71), Princeton, 1973 [=1963].
Plato. Complete Works. Edited with Introduction and Notes by John M. Cooper and D.S. Hutchinson, Indianapolis-Cambridge, 1997.

1.10. Plotinus
Plotini opera, ediderunt Paul Henry et Hans-Rudolf Schwyzer (Museum Lessianum, Series philosophica), tomus I, *Porphyrii Vita Plotini. Enneades I-III*; tomus II, *Enneades IV-V. Plotiniana arabica*, Paris-Bruxelles, 1951; 1959; tomus III, *Enneas VI*, Paris-Leiden, 1973 [= 'editio maior', H-S[1]].
Plotini opera ediderunt Paul Henry et Hans-Rudolf Schwyzer, tomus I, *Porphyrii Vita Plotini. Enneades I-III*; tomus II, *Enneades IV-V*; tomus III, *Enneas VI* (Scriptorum classicorum bibliotheca Oxoniensis), Oxonii, 1964; 1977; 1982 [= 'editio minor', H-S[2]].
Plotinus, with an English Translation by A.H. Armstrong (The Loeb Classical Library), in seven volumes, London-Cambridge, MA, 1966-88. This translation has been used for quotations.

1.11. Porphyrius
Porphyre, Sentences. Études d'introduction, texte grec et traduction française, commentaire, avec une traduction anglaise de John Dillon. Travaux édités sous la responsabilité de Luc Brisson (Histoire des doctrines de l'Antiquité classique, 33), Paris, 2005.

1.12. Simplicius
Simplicius. Commentaire sur le Manuel d'Épictète. Introduction et édition critique du texte grec par Ilsetraut Hadot (Philosophia antiqua, 66), Leiden-New York-Köln, 1996.
Simplicius. Commentaire sur le manuel d'Epictète. Tome I. Texte établi et

114   *Select Bibliography*

traduit par Ilsetraut Hadot (Collection des Universités de France), Paris, 2001.

1.13. Syrianus
Syriani in metaphysica commentaria, edidit Guilelmus Kroll (Commentaria in Aristotelem Graeca, vol. VI, pars I), Berlin, 1902.

2. Secondary literature

Amand, D. 1945. *Fatalisme et liberté dans l'antiquité grecque*, Louvain.
Beierwaltes, W. 1979. *Proklos. Grundzüge seiner Metaphysik* (Philosophische Abhandlungen, 24), Frankfurt am Main.
Bobzien, S. 1998. *Freedom and Determinism in Stoic Philosophy*, Oxford.
Boese, H. 1960: see above in Section 1.1.
Bonazzi, M. 2003. *Academici e Platonici. Il dibattito antico sullo scetticismo di Platone*, Milano.
Brittain, C. 2002. 'Attention Deficit in Plotinus and Augustine: Psychological Problems in Christian and Platonist Theories of the Grades of Virtues', in *Proceedings of the Boston Area Colloquium in Ancient Philosophy* 18, 223-63.
Brunner, F. 1997. 'De l'action humaine selon Proclus (De Providentia VI)', in Y. Gauthier (ed.), *Le dialogue humaniste* (Mélanges V. Cauchy), Montréal, 3-11.
——— 1992. 'L'idée de Kairos chez Proclus' in *Méthexis* (Mélanges E. Moutsopoulos), Athens, 173-181.
Cardullo, R.L. 1995. *Siriano – Esegeta di Aristotele. I: Frammenti e Testimonianze dei Commentari all'Organon*. Introduzione, Testo, Traduzione, Note e Commento (Symbolon, 14), Firenze.
Courcelle, P. 1974-5. *Connais-toi toi-même. De Socrate à Saint Bernard* (Études augustiniennes. Série Antiquité, 58-60), 2 vols, Paris.
D'Ancona, C. 2005. 'Les *Sentences* de Porphyre entre les *Ennéades* de Plotin et les *Éléments de Théologie* de Proclus' in L. Brisson (ed.), *Porphyre, Sentences*. Paris, 139-274.
Den Boeft, J. 1970. *Calcidius on Fate: His Doctrines and Sources* (Philosophia antiqua, 18), Leiden.
Deuse, W. 1973. *Theodoros von Asine: Sammlung der Testimonien und Kommentar* (Palingenesia, 6), Wiesbaden.
Dillon, J., & L.P. Gerson 2004. *Neoplatonic Philosophy: Introductory Readings*, Indianapolis.
Dillon, J., & A.A. Long (eds) 1988. *The Question of 'Eclecticism'. Studies in later Greek Philsophy* (Hellenistic Culture and Society, 3), Berkeley-Los Angeles-London.
Dillon, J. 1977. *The Middle Platonists: 80 BC to AD 220*, London (2nd edn 1996).
Dodds, E.R. 1963: see above in Section 1.1.
Dörrie, H. & M. Baltes 1993. *Der Platonismus in der Antike. Band 3: Der Platonismus im 2. und 3. Jahrhundert nach Christus*, Stuttgart-Bad Cannstatt.
Dragona-Monachou, M. 1994. 'Divine Providence in the Philosophy of the Empire' in *Aufstieg und Niedergang der Römischen Welt* II 36.7, Berlin-New York, 4417-90.
Dudley, J. 1999. *Diò e Contemplazione in Aristotele. Il Fondamento metafisico dell' 'Etica Nicomachea'* (Universita Cattolica del Sacro Cuore. Pubblicazioni del Centro di ricerche di metafisica. Temi metafisici e problemi del pensiero antico. Studi e testi, 76), Milano.
Erler, M. 1978: see above in Section 1.1

Select Bibliography

―――― 1980: see above in Section 1.1
Festugière, A.J. 1966-8: see above in Section 1.1
―――― 1970: see above in Section 1.1
Finamore, J.F. & J.M. Dillon 2002. *Iamblichus. De anima: Text, Translation, and Commentary* (Philosophia antiqua, 92), Leiden.
Gruber, J. 1978. *Kommentar zu Boethius, De consolatione Philosophiae* (Texte und Kommentare, 9), Berlin-New York.
Hadot, I. 2001: see above in Section 1.13
Hankinson, R.J. 1999. 'Determinism and Indeterminism', in K. Algra (ed.), *The Cambridge History of Hellenistic Philsophy*, Cambridge, 513-41.
Isaac, D. 1977: see above in Section 1.1
Johnston, S.I. 1990. *Hekate Soteria: A Study of Hekate's Roles in the Chaldaean Oracles and Related Literature* (American Classical Studies, 21), Atlanta.
Lautner, P. 2000. 'Iamblichus' Transformation of the Aristotelian *katharsis*, its Middle-Platonic Antecedents and Proclus' and Simplicius' Response to it' in *Acta Antiqua Academiae Scientiarum Hungariae* 40, 263-82.
Long, A.A., & D.N. Sedley 1987. *The Hellenistic Philosophers*, Cambridge.
Lovejoy, A.O. 1936. *The Great Chain of Being: A Study of the History of an Idea*, Cambridge, MA.
Majercik, R. 1989: see above in Section 1.4
Mansfeld, J. 1999. 'Alcinous on Fate and Providence' in J.J. Cleary (ed.), *Traditions of Platonism: Essays in Honour of John Dillon*, Aldershot, 139-50.
Marenbon, J. 2003. *Boethius* (Great Medieval Thinkers), Oxford.
Maurach, G. 1968. *Coelum Empyreum. Versuch einer Begriffsgeschichte*, Wiesbaden.
Mignuci, M. 1985. 'Logic and Omniscience, Alexander of Aphrodisias and Proclus', in *Oxford Studies in Ancient Philosophy* 3, 219-46.
O'Meara, D. 2003. *Platonopolis. Platonic Political Philosophy in Late Antiquity*, Oxford.
Opsomer, J. 1998. *In Search of the Truth. Academic Tendencies in Middle Platonism* (Verhandelingen van de Koninklijke academie voor wetenschappen, letteren en schone kunsten van België. Klasse der letteren, 163), Brussels.
Opsomer, J., & C. Steel 2003. *Proclus. On the Existence of Evils* (Ancient Commentators on Aristotle), London.
Pease, A.S. 1923. *M. Tulli Ciceronis De divinatione Libri Duo*, Urbana (reprinted: Darmstadt 1977).
Reis, B. 2000. 'Plotins großes Welttheater. Reflexionen zum Schauspielvergleich in *Enneade* III 2 [47]', in S. Gödde & Th. Heinze (eds), *Skenika: Beiträge zum antiken Theater und seiner Rezeption. Festschrift zum 65. Geburtstag von Horst-Dieter Blume*, Darmstadt, 291-311.
Russi, C. 2004. 'Le cause prossime plotiniane nell'esordio di *Enn.* III, 1 [3]: consonanze et dissonanze con la tradizione aristotelica', in *Elenchos* 25, 73-98.
Saffrey, H.D. 1992. 'Le thème du malheur des temps chez les derniers philosophes néoplatoniciens', in ΣΟΦΙΗΣ ΜΑΙΗΤΟΡΕΣ, *Chercheurs de sagesse: Hommage à Jean Pépin* (Études augustiniennes. Série Antiquité, 131), Paris, 421-31 [reprinted in H.D. Saffrey, *Le Néoplatonisme après Plotin II*, Paris, 2000, 207-17].
Saffrey, H.D., & L.G. Westerink (1968): see above in Section 1.1
Salles, R. 2005. *The Stoics on Determinism and Compatibilism* (Ashgate New Critical Thinking in Philosophy), Aldershot.
Schibli, H. 2002. *Hierocles of Alexandria*, Oxford.

Sedley, D. 1996. 'Three Platonist Interpretations of the *Theaetetus*', in C. Gill & M.M. McCabe (eds), *Form and Argument in Late Plato*, Oxford, 79-103.
Sharples, R.W. 1983. *Alexander of Aphrodisias: On Fate. Text, Translation and Commentary* (Duckworth Classical, Medieval and Renaissance Editions), London.
Sorabji, R. 1980. *Necessity, Cause and Blame. Aspects of Aristotle's Theory*, London.
—— 1983. *Time, Creation and the Continuum: Theories in Antiquity and the Early Middle Ages*, London.
—— 2004a. *The Philosophy of the Commentators 200-600 AD. A Sourcebook, Volume 1, Psychology*, London.
—— 2004b. *The Philosophy of the Commentators 200-600 AD. A Sourcebook, Volume 2, Physics*, London.
Steel, C. 1993. 'L'âme: modèle et image', in H.J. Blumenthal & E.G. Clark (eds), *The Divine Iamblichus. Philosopher and Man of Gods*, Bristol, 14-29.
—— 1999. 'Proclus on the Existence of Evil', in *Proceedings of the Boston Area Colloquium in Ancient Philosophy* 14, 83-102.
—— 2001. 'The Moral Purpose of the Human Body. A Reading of *Timaeus* 69-72', in *Phronesis* 46, 105-28.
—— 2003. 'Neoplatonic versus Stoic Causality: the Case of the Sustaining Cause ("sunektikon")', in C. Esposito & P. Porro (eds), *Quaestio 2. La Causalità*, Turnhout-Bari, 77-93.
—— 2005. 'Proclus' Defence of the *Timaeus* against Aristotle's Objections. A Reconstruction of a Lost Polemical Treatise', in Th. Leinkauf & C. Steel (eds), *Platons* Timaios – *Grundtext der Kosmologie / Plato's* Timaeus – *The Foundations of Cosmology* (Ancient and Medieval Philosophy, De Wulf-Mansion Centre, Series 1, 34), 163-93.
Strobel, B. 2007. *Vollständige Wiederherstellung des griechischen Textes von Proklos' Tria Opuscula* [work in progress].
Táran, L. 1975. *Academica: Plato, Philip of Opus, and the Pseudo-Platonic Epinomis* (Memoirs of the American Philosophical Society, 107), Philadelphia.
Thillet, P. 1984. *Alexandre d'Aphrodise: Traité du Destin. Texte traduit et établi* (Collection des Universités de France), Paris.
—— 2003. *Alexandre d'Aphrodise. Traité de la Providence. Version arabe de Abû Bišr Mattä ibn Yûnus*, Paris.
Tieleman, T. 1996. *Galen & Chrysippus on the Soul. Argument & Refutation in the De Placitis, Books II-III* (Philosophia antiqua, 68), Leiden-New York-Köln.
Van den Berg, B. 2001. *Proclus' Hymns. Essays, Translations, Commentary* (Philosophia antiqua, 90), Leiden-Boston-Köln.
Westerink, L.G. 1959. 'Exzerpte aus Proklos' Enneaden-Kommentar bei Psellos', in *Byzantinische Zeitschrift* 52, 1-10.
—— 1962. 'Notes on the 'Tria opuscula' of Proclus', in *Mnemosyne* 15, 159-68 [in the same volume: idem, Review of Boese (1960), 189-90].
Zambon, M. 2002. *Porphyre et le Moyen-Platonisme* (Histoire des doctrines de l'antiquité classique, 27), Paris.
Ziegler, K. 1934. 'Theodorus. 41. Mechaniker und Philosoph', in *RE*, 2. Reihe, 10. Halbband (= V A 2), col. 1860,47-1863,43.

Index of Passages

Texts quoted or alluded to by Proclus. References are to chapter and number of note in this edition.

ARCHIMEDES
  fr. 15,2 Heiberg: 25,117
ARISTOTLE
  An. Post. 1.2, 72b24: 30,138
  An. Post. 2.1, 89b24-5 and 34: 5,26
  DA 1.1, 403a10-12: 15,65
  EN 7.12, 1153a15-b11: 47,221
  EN 10.7, 1177a19-20 and
    1178a5-8: 47,222
  Metaph. 13.8, 1084b23ff.: 29,135
  Metaph. 14.3, 1090b19: 34,156
  Phys. 1.1, 185a11: 46,210
  Phys. 1.2, 185a1: 28,131
  Phys. 1.3, 186a9: 46,210
  Phys. 5.6, 230a31-b1: 11,50
CHALDEAN ORACLES (ed. des Places)
  passim: 1,4
  fr. 1,1: 32,150
  fr. 42,2: 42,188
  fr. 102: 11,52
  fr. 103: 21,98
  fr. 129,3: 4,21
  fr. 130: 21,100
  fr. 153: 21,99
  fr. 154: 21,99
  fr. 102: 21,97
  fr. [?]: 30,143
EPICTETUS
  Enchiridion 1.1ff.: 55,253
HERACLITUS
  fr. B 92: 1,3
HOMER
  Od. 12.453: 46,215
  Od. 19.163: 47,218
  Od. 20.17: 17,71
PLATO
  Alc. 135C6-10: 23,110
  Apol. 20E-23B: 48,224
  Apol. 21A6-7: 51,241
  Crat. 400C: 41,184
  Gorg. 466D8-E2: 57,258
  Gorg. 492E: 41,184
  Gorg. 492D-500D: 46,214
  Gorg. 493D5-6: 28,128; 66,287
  Gorg. 500D9-10: 47,216,220
  Gorg. 509A1-2: 46,212
  Leg. 1, 631D5: 45,207
  Leg. 4, 709B7-C3: 34,158
  Leg. 6, 783A1: 57,261
  Leg. 10, 892B1: 42,185
  Leg. 10, 904B: 35,163
  Parm. 130E4: 45,206
  Phaedo 65B3-4: 17,75
  Phaedo 65D: 17,76
  Phaedo 66B8ff.: 49,235
  Phaedo 66D7-8: 48,225 ; 49,230
  Phaedo 67C: 52,244
  Phaedo 67D1: 49,231
  Phaedo 68A1: 49,230
  Phaedo 70B10-C2: 66,285
  Phaedo 81B: 17,73
  Phaedo 82D3: 22,101
  Phaedo 87E1-2: 11,47
  Phaedr. 237B7-C2: 5,24
  Phaedr. 244A4-8: 19,89
  Phaedr. 244D3-4: 19,89
  Phaedr. 246C1-2: 24,115; 60,269
  Phaedr. 246E4-6: 24,114
  Phaedr. 247E2: 4,20
  Phaedr. 248C8: 3,15
  Phaedr. 250B2: 34,162; 41,182
  Phaedr. 252A5: 30,141
  Phaedr. 265D-266B: 29,133
  Phaedr. 265E1: 6,31
  Phil. passim: 46,214
  Phil. 16C5: 6,27

Phil. 26D7: 29,132
Phil. 40A-C: 17,74
Phil. 67B1-3: 46,213
Polit. 272E5-6: 11,51
Polit. 272E6: 13,60
Resp. 2, 379C5-6: 13,58
Resp. 3, 398A: 38,173
Resp. 4, 435E: 47,217
Resp. 5, 475B2-3: 45,209
Resp. 6, 510B7: 50,238
Resp. 6, 510B-511D: 28,129
Resp. 6, 511B6: 29,133; 50,238
Resp. 7, 533B8-C1: 48,227
Resp. 7, 533D4-6: 48,226; 50,237
Resp. 7, 534C1: 29,133
Resp. 7, 534E2-3: 29,134; 49,234
Resp. 9, 580E: 23,110
Resp. 9, 583B-588A: 46,214
Resp. 10, 588C-D: 47,219
Resp. 10, 617E3: 23,105
Soph. 249C6-8: 52,243
Symp. 184C6: 24,113
Theaet. 173E6-174A1: 49,233
Theaet. 176A: 3,14
Theaet. 187A5-6: 27,125
Tim. 27C1-3: 38,175
Tim. 27D6-28A1: 9,41
Tim. 29A5-6: 2,10
Tim. 30C8: 2,8
Tim. 35B2-7: 18,78
Tim. 37C1-3: 30,139
Tim. 40D: 1,4; 19,88
Tim. 41D4-5: 42,187
Tim. 41E2-3: 20,94
Tim. 42A3: 4,17
Tim. 42A5: 44,197
Tim. 48A1-2: 13,59
Tim. 53C2: 41,181
Tim. 62C-63B: 13,63
Tim. 66C6: 44,197
Tim. 68D4-7: 29,133
Tim. 89C5: 13,60
Epinomis: 50,239
Epinomis 992A1: 29,134
PLOTINUS
Enneads I 1 [53] 2,12-14: 26,121
Enneads I 1 [53] 9,12: 30,140
Enneads I 1 [53] 12-13: 16,67
Enneads I 2 [19] 8,13: 30,140
Enneads I 4 [46] 7,23ff.: 22,104
Enneads III 4 [15] 6,47-56: 22,102
Enneads V 3 [49] 3,44-5: 59,265
Enneads VI 9 [9] 10,11-12: 31,149

Index of Names

References are to chapters in the translation.

Apollo 3
Aristotle 5, 6, 15, 27, 28, 30, 31
Athenian stranger 42

Egypt 25
Epictetus 55

Greeks 38, 45

Homer 17

Iamblichus 1, 5, 53

Parmenides 4
Peripatetics 63
Persians 45, 47

Plato 1, 4, 5, 6, 11, 13, 21, 24, 27, 30, 31, 35, 42, 46, 49, 52, 60, 63
Platonists 5, 49
Plotinus 1, 5, 16, 53
Porphyry 5
Pythia 51, 52

Socrates 4, 6, 29, 49, 50, 51, 52
Stoics 63, 66
Sybil 19
Syrianus (our teacher) 66

Theodore 1
Theodore of Asine 53
Thracians 47
Timaeus 42

Index of Subjects

References are to chapters and notes of the translation. See also the summary of Proclus' argument in the Introduction, pp. 26-34.

act prior to potency, n. 195
apatheia, 27, n. 126
appetitive (desirous) faculty
   (*epithumêtikon/horektikon*), 16,
   47, 59, n. 66, nn. 106-7
  not separable from body, 16
  distinction between appetitive
   and cognitive faculty, 58
arithmetic, 18, 28, 29, 41, 43, n. 83
astrological interpretation of fate, n. 37
autenergêtos, self-activated, n. 256
autexousion, see self-determination
autoperigraptos, self-determined, n. 256
autoptic, see intuitive

Bacchic experience, n. 87
boulêsis, see will

causes
  three causes of events: divine
   providence, fate and human
   skill, 34
  efficient causes are distinct from
   their effects, 8, n. 38
  active cause are incorporeal, n. 61
celestial bodies, their influence, n. 170, n. 174
choice (*proairesis*),
  possibility, 35, 36
  we are masters of our actions
   because we are masters of our
   choice, 36
  characteristic of rational life
   opposed to sense perception, 44
  dialectical definition, 58-9
  a rational faculty that strives for
   some good, either true or
   apparent, 60
  a dual ambivalent faculty, 60
  different from will, 57, 60, n. 258
  bodies lack this capacity, 13, 44,
   n. 62, n. 201
  animals without choice, n. 262
  misfortune of good people not
   argument against free choice,
   53-5
common notions (*koinai ennoiai*), 6,
  n. 28, n. 30
  of providence and fate, 7-8, n. 34
  Stoic origin, n. 28
contingent events (*endekhomena*)
  not everything is necessitated, 63
  nature of contingency, n. 274
  divine knowledge of future
   contingents, 62-5
contemplation (*theôria*)
  possible for the incarnated soul, 5,
   49, n. 121, n. 232
contemplative life, n. 236
convention, opposition with nature,
  45, n. 204
criteria of truth, 44, n. 198

Delphic maxim: know yourself, n. 164
Determinism, universe a
  deterministic system, 2
dialectic
  contributing to knowledge of
   essences, 6, 58
  making the one multiple, the
   multiple one, 29
  coping-stone of the sciences, 29
  using analysis, synthesis, division
   and demonstration, 30

interconnection of sciences, 29, 50
method of dialectic, n. 130, n. 133, n. 136
divination, 37-9
  human beings lovers of divination, 37
  two types, n. 177
dokêsis, uncertain opinion about the good, n 258
drama of human life, 2, n. 6, n. 161

eph' hêmin, see what depends on us
epibolê, see intuition
eternity, time
  three levels: eternal in substance and activities, temporal in substance and activities, eternal in substance, temporal in activities, 9
  time as image of eternity, n. 56
  time: eternal or limited, n. 41
  fate concerns activities in place and time, 10
ether, the soul does not emanate from ether, 42
ethereal heaven, n. 188
evil
  coloured by the good, n. 272
  evil is infirm, 26
  evil not wanted: nobody chooses it knowingly, 57, n. 260
  soul has ambivalent inclination to good and evil, 57
external accidents of life not important, 22

fate
  as connection (*heirmos*) of all events, 2, 7, 10, 13, n. 34
  identical with providence according to Theodore, 2
  distinguished from providence, 3-5, 5-15
  common notion of fate, 7-8
  fate identical with nature, 11-12, n. 50, n. 51, n. 53
  fate as cause transcends the events subject to it, 8
  things connected by fate are corporeal and temporal, 10
  corresponds to the vegetative power of the soul, 11
  fate subordinated to providence, 13-14
  fate something divine, not god, 14
  spindle as metaphor of fate, n. 37
  rational soul intermediary: sometimes subject to fate, sometimes above fate, 20
  see also: providence, soul
flower of the intellect, 32
freedom
  divine privilege according to Theodore, 56
  human freedom not absolute, 56, 61, n. 166, n. 270
  only the virtuous is free, 23
  share of freedom corresponding to share of virtue, 24
  willing slavery greatest freedom, 24
  see also: choice
foreknowledge
  foreknowledge of future events helpful, 38-9
  divine foreknowledge, 62-5
future
  human curiosity about the future, 37-9
  knowledge of future events, 62-5

geometry, 18, 28, 29, 41, 43, n. 64, n. 83
gods
  monads of the gods, 19
  the gods know future events in a determinate way, 63-5
  will, power and good identical, n. 268
  god source of good, 34
  freedom is a divine privilege (Theodore), 56
  hypercosmic gods, 19
  providence resides primitively in the gods, n. 35
  revelations of the gods, 1
  union with the god (the One), 31
  soul becoming godlike, 32, 60

heavens, empyrean, ethereal, n. 188
Hecate, Rhea, 42, n. 189
hedonism, discussion of, 45-7, n. 214
heimarmenê, see fate
human action part of the universe, 34, 35

Indexes

human customs, diversity explained by referring to different lives of soul, 47

ignorance, Socratic ignorance implies a form of knowledge, 48, 51-2
initiation rituals, n. 82
intellect
    godlike intellect above the soul, 19
    much praised, n. 36
    intellect as leader, n. 207
    supreme principle for Aristotle, 31
intellection
    above reason, 19
    beyond science, 30
intellectual life versus sensible life, 44
intelligible versus sensible, 14
intermediary
    needed in the procession, 20, n. 95
    rational soul as intermediary, 20, 60, 61, n. 242, n. 266
intuition
    mystical intuition, 19
    epibolê, n. 137
    autoptic knowledge, 30, n. 137
    see also: intellection
irascible faculty, n. 66, n. 71
    not separable from body, 16-17, 47, n. 66

kairos, 34, n. 157
knowledge (*gnôsis, epistêmê*),
    two types of knowledge: one of the incarnated soul, one of the soul when released from the body, 3-5, 49
    five different modes of knowledge (opinion, mathematical, dialectical, intuitive, divine madness, 27-32, n. 245
    knowledge by touching, 30-1
    similar known by similar, 31, n. 147
    the mode of knowledge must not correspond to what the object is, but to what the subject is, 63
kolophôn, n. 273

licence and power (*exousia*) to do all things, 60-1, n. 267
life
    three types of life corresponding to three parts of the soul, 47, n. 217
    one vital force penetrating the universe on all levels, 40
light, metaphor of light, n. 32

madness, divine madness of the soul, 19, 31, n. 89
mathematical sciences, 18, 28, 29, 41, 43
    are they really sciences?, 50
merit, n. 248
    see also: recompense of merit
metriopatheia, moderation of the passions, 27, n. 126
misfortune, of good people not an argument against free choice, 53-5
Moirai, 7, 33, n. 37, n. 153
motion
    distinction between unmoved (*akinêton*), self-moved (*autokinêton*), externally moved (*eterokinêton*), 4, n. 16
    all bodies externally moved, 10, 11
mystical intuition, 19

nature
    definition of nature, 12
    versus convention, 45, n. 20
    nature does nothing in vain, n. 171
    nature identical with fate, 11-12, n. 50, n. 51, n. 53
    see also: vice (against nature)
necessity, identical with fate, 13

ôdis, labour of mind and its fruits, concepts, n. 1
One
    first principle of all, 29, 31
    union of the soul with the One, n. 146
    the One of the soul, 31
opinion (*doxa*)
    grasping the truth without its cause, 27, nn. 124-5
    see also: dokêsis
optical illusion, n. 70
oracles
    our interest in oracles, 33
    utility of oracles, 38

do not remove our responsibility, 38-9
oracle of Apollo to Laius, 38
oracle of the Pythia to Socrates, 51-2
oracles on how to escape from fate, 21
Chaldean Oracles, n. 5 (*see also* Index of Passages)
orders of beings,
   intellectual, psychic and corporeal, 9
   two reigns: intelligible and sensible, 14

parapêgma: astronomical clock, n. 279
passion, affection (*pathos*), 23-4, 47, n. 126, n. 197
   see also: *apatheia*, *metriopatheia*
periopê, vantage-point as metaphor, 18, 19, n. 84
persecution of Proclus, 22, n. 103
play, versus seriousness, 3, 43, n. 11, n. 196
pleasurable
   not identical with the good, 45-7
   divergent opinions and customs, 45-7
prayers
   not in vain, 38
   use, n. 172
(*pro*)*airesis*, *see* choice
procession, leaves no void, always through intermediaries, 9, 20, n. 42, n. 95
providence (*pronoia*),
   identical with fatal necessity (Theodore), 2
   common notion of providence, 7-8
   providence transcends as a cause that which is subject to it, 8
   definition of providence: source of good things, 13
   providence a divine cause, god *per se*, 13, 14, n. 35
   fate subordinated to providence, 13-14
   providence superior to intellect, 13
   providence before intellect (*pro-noia*), n. 34
   misfortune of good people poses difficulty for doctrine of providence, 53-5
purification of the soul, 27, 49, n. 232
rational soul, *see* soul
recompense of merit, 54-5, n. 250
relation (*skhesis*), according to disposition or relation opposed to according to substance, 20, n. 93, n. 202
relativism of the good, 45-7
responsibility, 33-6
   responsibility for actions threefold: divine providence, fate, human action, 34-5
   responsibility for good or bad life, 54
   see also: 'what *depends* on us'
rest and peace of the soul, n. 143
Rhea, Hecate, n. 189
rituals of priests can have some influence on the outcome, 38-9

scepticism, discussion of sceptic arguments about knowing the truth, 48-52
sciences
   sciences distinguished from sense perception, 43
   see also: mathematical sciences and dialectic
self-determination (*autexousion*), 4, 23, n. 166, n. 270
   just a word, not a human reality (Theodore), 2
   in strict sense, divine privilege, 56-61
   see also: *autoperigraptos*
self-knowledge, 30, 41, n. 164
self-love (*philautia*), n. 155
self-movement, n. 16, n. 256
self-reflection, corporeal and sensible powers incapable of it, 41, 44, n. 183
sense perception
   lowest level of knowledge, dim image of knowledge, linked to the body
   via organs, not self-reflective, 41, 44
   opposition between sciences and knowledge based on sense perception, 43
   critique of sensible knowledge, 44

Indexes

sensible life dominated by fate, 44
sensible versus intelligible realm, 14
serious, *see* play
ship, metaphor of the ship and the storm, 22, n. 102
silence of the soul, n. 149
slavery
  willing slavery (*ethelodouleia*) greatest freedom, 24, n. 113
  see also: freedom
sôrites, n. 286
soul
  two types of soul, one separable from body, one inseparable, 3-5, 15-26
  superior versus inferior parts of the soul, 23
  threefold division of soul, vegetative, sensitive and rational, n. 48
  vegetative soul, 11
  sensitive faculty not separable from body, 16
  appetitive and irascible faculty not separable from body, 16
  rational soul: its twofold activities, one related to the ordering of irrational life, 17; one reverted upon itself, 18
  soul as a rational world, n. 79
  finds in itself reasons of all things, 17, 43, 44
  rational soul as intermediary, 20, 60, 61
  intermediary between sense perception and intellect, n. 203, n. 242, n. 266
  examine the soul when it is in accordance with nature, 22-6
  diverse types of human life explained by dominance of different parts of soul, 47
  source of souls, 42
  classes of souls, n. 116
  cloths of the soul, n. 108
  dance of souls, 34, n. 162
  divine souls, 19, 24, 34
  descent of the soul, n. 108
  the undescended soul: Plotinus' thesis and the controversy in the school, n. 121, n. 232
Sybil, n. 90
sumpatheia, in the world, n. 43, n. 55

tekhnê, human skill as one of three causes contributing to an event, 34
Theodore
  his questions on fate and providence, 1
  old friend of Proclus, 1
  his deterministic world view, 2
  an engineer who understands the world as a mechanical clock, 2
  mathematics, his discipline, 18
  implicit reference to Archemides, 25
  a lover of philosophy and versed in mathematical learning, 41
  maker of astronomical clock, 65
theologians, 1, 21, 31
theôria, *see* contemplation
theurgy, 38, 39, n. 52, n. 99, n. 178
time, *see* eternity
touch (*epaphê*, *thixis*), knowledge by touching, 30-1

universe
  universe as a deterministic system (Theodore), 2
  human action part of the universe, 34, 35
  corporeal world a fully interconnected system, 10
  nothing 'epeisodic', n. 156
  see also: *sumpatheia*
upward stature of man, n. 211

vice, infirmity of the soul, no power, state against nature, 20, 24, 26, n. 111, n. 120
virtue, 22-5, 61
  virtue alone is free (*adespoton*), 23, 24, n. 105, n. 126
  the virtuous is not slave to fate, 22
vital force permeating universe, 40-4

what depends on us (*eph' hêmin*)
  is only a name, not a reality (Theodore), 2
  right definition, 56-61
  opinion of the ancients, 57
  is situated in our interior choices and impulses, not in what happens outside, 35
  Epictetus teaches us how to distinguish what depends on

us from what depend
on us, 55
is a capacity of choice, 36
is identical with the faculty of
choice, 57-9
is not a power or licence to do all
things, 60
supplementary arguments to
prove that it exists, 66
will (*boulêsis*), different from choice,
57, 60, n. 258